MEMORIALS OF ASH PRIORS

BY

ARTHUR WILFRID BAYNHAM, M.A.

Vicar of the Parish.

JAMES G. COMMIN

230 High Street Exeter

1908

Dedication

TO MY PARISHIONERS

IN THE HOPE THAT IT MAY BE FOUND TO
CONTAIN SOME USEFUL AND INTERESTING
INFORMATION

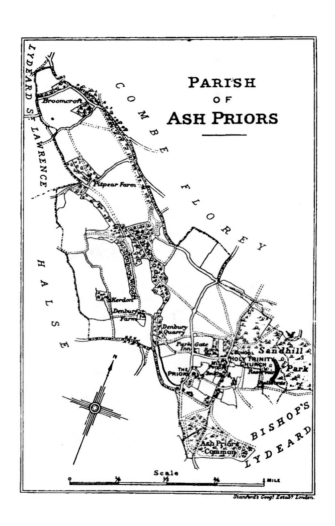

PARISH

OF

ASH PRIORS

Scale

Stanford's Geogl Estab! London.

PREFACE

I HAVE to thank those who have helped me in writing this little book. Sir Wroth P. C. Lethbridge for an introduction to Mr. Arthur Humphreys, who kindly put me in the way of consulting some valuable sources of information respecting the ancient history of the place, also for letting me see Sir Roper Lethbridge's little book and pedigree of the Lethbridge family. Sir Prior Goldney has not only assisted me with the loan of books, but also with the store of knowledge which he carries with him. Mr. J. Houghton Spencer has given me much information respecting the Church. Mr. T. Clarke, from his intimate connection with the family, has rendered me much assistance in my account of the Lethbridge family. I am indebted to Mr. R. W. Marston for his translation of the "Compotus" and for explanation of the terms which occur therein.

The principal books which I have consulted and from which I have frequently quoted are Collinson's *History of Somerset; The History of Taunton*, by James Savage; *English Village Communities*, by F. Seebohm; *English Architecture*, by Thomas Dinham Atkinson; *The Title Deeds of the Church of England*, by T. Garnier; The Rev. H. T. Ellacombe's *Bells of Somerset; The History of Taunton Priory*, by Thomas Hugo.

MEMORIALS OF ASH PRIORS

INTRODUCTION

I T has been said, "If there were no written histories of our country we should be able to construct one from things as they are. The past is summed up in the state of things as we find them to-day. But it is especially from words employed in the denomination of places and physical features of the country that we may glean a knowledge of the past. All such words are or were at one time significant, and if we can determine their meaning they help us to construct something of our history." It is so in the case of this little village, it being one of three places in the county of Somerset which take their name from the sort of trees which abound in the district.

It is thought that before the Norman conquest, when the ancient British Christians worshipped in little wattled churches, in many places there would be nothing but a little hut, containing a font, placed most probably under some large tree under which the strolling preacher was in the habit of taking up his position when preaching to the people. In course of time a stone cross would be erected, and hence we have the village or churchyard cross, on the steps of which the preacher stood, as his predecessors had stood under the tree. A tree has always marked a spot, and served as it does to this day as a place of meeting, and carrying on business, pitching camps and holding courts. You may see this everywhere in India. The judge when he goes on tour through the districts, pitches his tent under the shade of a great tree. He holds his court under a tree in the open air. The traveller rests under the shade of a tree during the heat of the day, because in the daytime it is always cool under a tree. If he sleeps in the open he chooses a tree, for under a tree it is always dry and warm at night. If he died in the districts far away from a burying ground he was buried under a tree. The natives set up their gods under trees. In connection with these remarks I will mention an incident which occurred one evening when I was sitting writing this account of Ash Priors. A man was shown in to me who had come to see me on very important business, one who had lately left the parish and gone to live where the Knights Templars formerly had their hostel. " Well ! " I said, " where are you living now ? " " At Stalford," he replied. " Where is that ? " " Between here and Halse, on the bounds of the two parishes." " How do you get there ? " " You go along the road to Halse," he said, " and turn up the lane on the right hand by the ' old ash.' " " Ah ! there you are," I said, " that is just the illustration I want for my book." The tree referred to is an old ivy clad ash just opposite the turning.

The identical tree from which the place took its name must have disappeared long ago. The tree shown in the photograph is merely a typical ash tree on the roadside, which I leave my readers to identify.

Ash Priors, no doubt, derived its name from the

The Ash *(Fraxinus Excelsior)*.

The Old Parish Chest.

tree. It may have been the prevalence of the trees in the parish. Now I am bound to say that the ash is not met with in anything like the same numbers that it is in some other parts of the country and possibly in the county. It is not for the ash so much as for the oak and the elm that we tremble when the winter storms sweep up the valley from the Bristol Channel and "roar in the tops of the elms and hiss in the pines"; but walk through Ash Wood and then you will understand from the abundance of ash saplings that once upon a time there must have been a forest of ash trees in the parish. From these ash saplings which are kept periodically cut down the owner of the wood derives no small profit by the sale of hurdles made from them on the spot, by skilled workmen, and sold at 9d. apiece. It need not have been from the prevalence of the ash that the place got its name, but from some one particular tree, so one place came to be called Oak, another Ash, and a third Elm. It may have been that at this tree public meetings were usually held, or it may have become noted for some incident with which it was associated, as in the instance of the tree under which Augustine invited the bishops of the British church to a conference with a view to inducing them to conform to the Roman practice of the observance of Easter and those other points in which it differed from the use of Western Christendom, at a place in Gloucestershire hard by the Severn, since known as Augustine's Oak.

There are some fine specimens of beech on the highlands. Sandhill Park abounds in oaks, and there are one or two old wrecks which tell of heavy gales from the south-west. Once the Admiralty had an eye to some of them to repair the wooden walls of England, and they sent their agent down to buy. A bargain was struck, and the trees were felled, but they proved to be not so sound as they looked, being rotten at the core. As the trees were being hauled through the park, cutting up the coach drive, and doing no end of damage, Sir Thomas Lethbridge remonstrated, and insisted upon their being taken round another way at much trouble and additional expense. The agent seeing an opportunity of getting off his bargain which had proved so disappointing, availed himself of it, and left the trees for Sir Thomas to dispose of to someone else.

The position of the village also points to its antiquity. The Church and the group of the oldest houses, standing as they do upon the rising ground, and founded upon the rock just above all that low lying ground which, before it was drained, as indeed it is now in wet weather, was often, if not flooded, at least a marsh. The builders of those days were wiser in more ways than one, building their houses upon rising ground on the moors, which were practically islands, or on the slopes of hills which afforded a firm foundation as well security from their enemies, and it is due to this marshy nature of the ground in spite of drainage that the Common owes its existence.

The origin of the name and the position of the village suggests the existence of the place from the earliest times; our history however, commences in the time of King Alfred. At that time this parish formed a part of the Manor of Bishops Lydeard. I need not tell again the old stories of Alfred and the cakes, or of how he disguised himself as a minstrel and went as a spy into the camp of the Danes, but it is a part of the legitimate history of Ash Priors to relate how that at the time when Alfred was thus engaged he left his children in charge of a learned man named Asser, who was rewarded by the king for his faithful services with the gift of the Manors of Wellington, West Buckland and Bishops Lydeard. This man became Bishop of Sherborne, where he died in 883, and upon his death these manors were conferred on Athelm, first Bishop of Wells, and remained as part of the endowment of that See under fourteen bishops in succession, down to Bishop Giso, who was consecrated on 4 April, 1059. In the time of Edward the Confessor, Ash is still part of the Manor of Bishops Lydeard, and belonged to the church of Wells, but it was taken from the church by Harold, Earl of Kent and Wessex, and was not restored to the church, for though at the death of Harold, William the Conqueror restored Harold's other estates to the church of Wells, he conferred the Manor of Ash upon Roger Arundel, one of his attendants into England.

At the time of Edward the Confessor, about 1063, at the extreme western limit of the hundred of Taunton Dean came that of Kingsbury West, an area comprising the parishes of Wiveliscombe, Fitzhead, Bishops Lydeard and Ash, known in those days as Esse, spelt in old documents variously as Eise, Aissa, Aish and Aixe, and afterwards when the Priors of Taunton came to possess the manor, as Esse Prioris or Ash Priors. It then consisted of three hides and one yardland, a hide being one hundred and twenty acres, according to the Dane geld, or tax, imposed by the Danes, a yardland being about fifteen acres. The hundred was an ancient territorial division among the Teutonic races; but whether this division of the country into hundreds has reference to the fact that it originally contained a hundred families, or a hundred warriors, or a hundred manors is uncertain. To get a bird's-eye view of the hundred of Kingsbury West you may ascend Cothelstone Hill, and looking back you will have it.

Roger de Arundel received many favours from William the Conqueror, no doubt in recognition of his services at the memorable battle of Hastings, in which he led the centre of William's army. According to the Norman survey, at the end of the recital of lands belonging to the Church of Wells, Roger Arundel holds Aissa of the King "injuste." Sawin held it in the time of King Edward, of the Bishop of Wells. A further account of this manor is given in Doomsday, "Roger himself holds Aixe." Ailric held it in the time of King Edward and gelded for two hides. "The arable is four caracutes, in demesne is one caracute,* and three servants and five villanes and five cottagers† with two ploughs. There are eight acres of meadow and ten acres of wood. Pasture two furlongs long and one furlong broad. It is worth twenty shillings."

This Roger de Arundel was third son of Roger de Montgomery, a town in Normandy, upon whom the Conqueror bestowed the Earldom of Arundel and Shrewsbury, and took his name from the Castle of Arundel, his father's residence. He had two sons, Gilbert the elder, from whom descended in direct line the present Lord Arundel of Wardour in Wiltshire, and Robert, his second son, on whom he bestowed the Manor of Ash; and it was he who gave two hides of land with the Church of Aissa and its dependencies to the Priory of Taunton.

---

*As much land as one team could plough in a year.

†One who lived on the Common without paying rent or having land of his own.

GENERAL DESCRIPTION OF
THE PARISH

ASH PRIORS, a small, but by no means insignificant village in the County of Somerset, is situated at the head of the beautiful vale of Taunton, commonly called Taunton Dean, or the town on the river Tone, in a woody valley, the word Dean being applied to forests. Six miles north-west of Taunton and less than a mile from Bishops Lydeard Station on the Minehead and West Somerset Branch of the Great Western Railway, it is easy of access. The area of the parish given in a valuation list dated 19 Dec., 1862, is 612 a. 3 r. 2 p. The rateable value £1080 1s. 6d. Gross estimated rental £1169 11s. 2d. The parish consists of 36 houses, 12 others actually in the parish of Bishops Lydeard practically go with Ash Priors, and two with Lydeard S. Lawrence.

The parishes dovetail into one another in such a manner that though some of the houses have been transferred to the civil parish of Ash Priors they remain in the ecclesiastical parish of Bishops Lydeard. By the Local Government Board order 16,397 which came into force on the 24 March, 1884, the north and south lodges of Sandhill Park were added to Bishops Lydeard and Denbury Farm was transferred to Ash Priors. The names of the different properties given in the same list are:—Part of Sandhill Park and Lodges, The Priory, Rock House, Ash Farm, Denbury Farm, Pitpear Farm,

The Park Gate Inn, Ash Mills, Ballifants, Lidwells, Ash Wood, Kirton, Queen's Bridge, part of Greenway, Piley, Broomcroft, Ash Common, Durboro and Bartrims, Smith's shop and garden. The houses are built of stone with thatched roofs, many of them having been small farm houses in former days. The climate is particularly mild, and the soil very productive. A better description of the situation and surroundings will not be found than that given in the words of a poem by Dr. Thomas Amory, a native of Taunton, published in 1824.

> Tall bushy trees, o'er all the region found
> With cooling shades refresh the fertile ground.
>
> .   .   .   .   .   .
>
> Gay painted blossoms smile on lower trees,
> With promised nectar thirsty palates please,
> And with their sweets perfume the vernal breeze.
> While warbling birds melodious notes employ,
> At once exalt, and tell, the Shepherd's joy.
> Here fruitful hillocks swell amidst the plain,
> In verdure clad, and rich in future grain ;
> Adown whose sides the murmuring torrents roll,
> To charm the muse, to bless the poet's soul,
> And, all around, proud guardian hills ascend,
> Whose height from winds inclement well defend.

It would be difficult to find a spot in the county so well favoured as this little village, both with natural advantages as well as modern conveniences, objects of interest in the immediate neighbourhood, scope for scientific pursuits and the study of archæology and opportunities for recreation, whilst at the same time an ideal place for retirement and a quiet life. There is a suggestion in the name Ash Priors of its past history, of a religious atmosphere of monastic retirement, and it still looks its name. Off the high road it is clear of the dust of our times, apart from the bustle and vulgarity of the world, like "the plain called ease" in the immortal allegory wherein Christian "walked with much content." Close at hand is some of the most romantic and wildest scenery in Somersetshire.

In the valley are rich pastures, sheltered home-steads and fruitful orchards, to the value of which the people are fully alive. They understand the culture of the apple tree, pruning, grafting, and cider making, packing and storing. Naturally the art of gardening comes to people who live in so rich a valley.

There is no public charity, and I think it may be said there is no real poverty in the parish. Most of the men earn good wages as coachmen, grooms, gardeners, carpenters, and working on the estate in various other capacities. There are a few farm labourers. The now disused quarries and lime kilns in Ash Wood tell of the days when there was more land under cultivation and railroads were not made, when the demand for lime to fertilize the fields for corn growing was greater than it is now. It was in this occupation that William Clements met his untimely death, by the falling in of a stone quarry, in the month of August, 1832.

The village lies on a sunny slope to the north of the Common, from either end of which a pretty view of it is obtained, with its cottages and farm buildings backed by the tall beech trees in Sandhill Park, the home of the rooks, and surrounded by the Quantocks, the Blackdown, and the Brendon Hills. The Parsonage House appears at its best from the Common through the trees. The Church tower, a plain red structure, compared with its graceful neighbour at Bishops Lydeard, is a conspicuous object rising above the trees. The Priory, with its grounds, requires a closer

inspection for which you must pass through the village.
From its modest position at the foot of the hill you
might pass it by unnoticed. It is here, however, that
the chief interest in the history of the parish centres;
whence it derives its name besides from ancient forests
of ash trees, if, from Mr. Montgomery's account of the
neighbouring parish of Halse, where he speaks of " This
little parish of hazel beeches being shut in in the
days of King Alfred by oak on one side and waving
forests of ash on the other," we may gather a reference
to Ash Priors.

The field names of the parish form a valuable clue
to many points of parish history, indeed from them
we can almost arrive at a general knowledge of the
history of the place. To give a list of the names of
184 plots of ground, would be of little value without
the tithe map to point out their position. There is
no saying how long the ancient enclosures have been
called by the names by which they are known to-
day; some of them are evidently called after former
tenants, some from their higher or lower position
and the nature of the ground, some from their former
connection with the Church. There are 23 acres and
2 roods which are still called The Parsonage Lands,
the Parsonage Barn and Yard, the Parsonage Mead.
There are 35 acres of common on the west side of
the stream which runs across it. Among those fields
called after persons are:

Dawe's Four Acres	Durborow's Mead
Shelves Orchard	Tarr's Field
Frian's Croft	Chick's Garden
Cotton's Close	Ifords
Ash Close	Hill's Home Mead
Myhill's Moor	Horsey's Mead

Bartram's Mead	Upper and Lower Knowls
Lang's Orchard	Upper and Lower Lidwells
Nations	Furze Close
Milton's Meads	Holmes
Pan Close	Batsham Mead

The next list is one of the inhabitants of Ash Priors for the tax levied in 1643, and the sums of money are the amount paid to the Long Parliament.

ASH PRIORS, IN 1642-1643.

Edward Cook, clerk	15s.	9d.
Elinor Ballifant	7s.	
Elizabeth Mantle	3s.	6d.
Edward Dollen	4s.	10d.
Anthony Pile...	12s.	
James Kingston		6d.
William Nayshon	4s.	8d.
Christopher Kiste	2s.	6d.
Richard Tucker	2s.	4d.
Johan Kist ...	4s.	6d.
James Basley...	2s.	
Johan Lambly	2s.	6d.
John Webber	1s.	6d.
Symon Castle...	2s.	
William Kerswell	11s.	4d.
Agnes Dawe, widow	3s.	6d.
Katherine Bartram	4s.	6d.
Henrie Copner	3s.	
Agnes Courtis, widow ...	2s.	6d.
William Morle	1s.	6d.
Johan Rossiter		8d.
Maris Boyce ...	3s.	
William Battinge	4s.	6d.
Henrie White	1s.	
Nicholas Syndercombe...	5s.	

Thomas Ballifant	...	...	1s.	6d.
John Steeven	...	...		6d.
Henry Hoyle	...	...	1s.	
Jeffery White	...	...	1s.	
Elizabeth Byshop, widow		...	1s.	
Elizabeth Seaman, widow		...		6d.

From this list we arrive at the conclusion that the house known as "Ballifants" was an old house before Sandhill Park, at least as we know it, was built, and is probably a good deal older than 1643. It was called after the family of which Thomas Ballifant was then the representative.

Dawe's Four Acres belonged to Agnes Dawe, widow, and Bartrams to Catherine Bartram. It is a curious fact that the only name in the list which still survives in the parish is "Webber," a family who do not claim Ash Priors as their home.

The Rev. Edward Cook was then apparently incumbent of the parish.

There were many widows in Ash Priors in those days. This may be accounted for by the fact that the country was at that time engaged in civil war.

Whether this is a complete list of names of the inhabitants of the place at that period or not, it at any rate gives the names of those persons who were rich enough to be taxed. Of the names which occur in the registers at the beginning of the 18th century, the most frequent are given below. The name Ballifant does not appear in the registers of Ash Priors, but it occurs in those of Bishops Lydeard.

Bryant	Milton	Hemboro	Furse
Fouracre	Winter	Hucklebridge	Ash
Hill	Blake	Tarr	Nation
Middleton	Horsey	Trott	Hallet

The following schedule probably refers to the census taken at the commencement of the last century :—

A return made by John Hurford, overseer of the poor of the parish of Ash Priors, in the county of Somerset, to the Justices, on the 13 day of April, 1801.

Houses inhabited, 29. Uninhabited, 1. Families, 37. Males, 70. Females, 85. Total, 155. Occupations: Agricultural, 39. Trades, 11. Others not employed in the two previous classes, 105. This was the first census.

The rise and fall of the population may be seen from the following returns.

Census	1801	...	155	Census	1881	...	191
„	1831	...	201	„	1891	...	128
„	1861	...	207	„	1901	...	111
„	1871	...	212				

In 1876 the following names appear :—

Vicar ...	Rev. V. C. Day, M.A., Oxon.
Ash Farm	Mr. John Blackmore.
Park Gate Inn...	... George Knight.
School Mistress	Miss Louise Pullin.
The Priory	... J. Winter, Esqre.
Wheelwright ...	... Edward Hobbs.
Blacksmith ...	... William Hobbs.
Miller ...	... Edwin Lockyer.
Shoe Maker ...	... George Stevens.
Shop Keeper ...	... Thomas Stevens.
Ballifant's Farm	... Henry Woolcott.
Pitpear	... Mr. John Skinner.
Church Clerk ...	... Thomas Hobbs.

The village is supplied with good water from a pump which draws from a spring yielding an unfailing supply, the overflow of which goes to swell the stream which divides the parishes of Bishops Lydeard and

Ash Priors, and which as recently as 1876 used to turn the mill wheel. This spring rises in an orchard belonging to the Sandhill Estate. Where water is scarce the water courses are a frequent source of litigation, and over this spring there has been much contention, so much so that it became the subject of fierce dispute between the Lethbridges and the Winters, which raged for years, and there was seldom an assize when the case did not appear. It engaged the attention of some of the first lawyers of the day, ending eventually in a compromise between Sir Thomas Lethbridge and Mr. John Winter, on 12 April, 1845, when a wall was built at the spring, the water being conducted in the direction of the village through a subterranean aqueduct through the hill, in some places at a great depth. The stream which flows in the opposite direction supplies Sandhill Park, and crosses the road at Greenway. The story is told how on one of these occasions Sir Thomas was asked at what he valued the spring? " I understand," said the lawyer, "that you have already spent some thousands of pounds over it." " True," replied the Baronet, "and I would spend as much again."

The stream, which passes under the culvert and crosses the Common, joins the Halse Water and Wooddean, and eventually flows into the Tone, into which all the local streams find their way.

The earliest mention of the Mill, as far as I have been able to ascertain, is in the Bailiff's Account with the Prior of Taunton in the year, 1439, and it has probably been there ever since Ash Priors became a manor. It is not mentioned in Doomsday, but it is not likely that the Lord of the Manor would allow his tenants to grind at another lord's mill. There is no longer heard the hum of the mill stones racing round, and the splash of the water on the great over-shot wheel at the back. It is a small stream which rises in the parish at Pitpear, gathers strength from springs at Denbury, only to lose it again by a stream which separates the parish from Halse. The stream which comes to Ash Priors has the appearance of being artificially diverted from Denbury through Queensbridge and the Priory Grounds, and thence again obviously diverted from what would have been its natural course, being kept by a wall along the higher ground, so as to run into the pond above the Mill which is not only filled by a stream which would naturally have taken a different course, but considerably supplemented by the aqueduct from Sandhill, and thus the Mill was made possible.

Without all this engineering not a drop of water would have come near it, or at any rate with sufficient elevation and power to work it. No one would imagine that it was a mill stream which runs down the village under the culvert and across the Common. Yet it supplied sufficient power to work the Mill, and when the pond was full would keep it going all day.

The old house overlooking the pond gives the appearance of great age; there are some very large stones worked into the building which probably have a previous history. It was here that John Tarr lived quite recently, although the name is one of the oldest in the parish, and will be noticed as the name of one of the tenants in the Bailiff's Account with the Prior of Taunton in Esse. Mr. Tarr was a man who could put his hand to anything and did a lot of work in the parish. Among other things he was a gardener, and every year in springtime we are reminded of his skill in grafting and the choice of a good strain of pink May when he grafted those two trees with the deep rose coloured bloom which attract so much attention.

The view of the mill-pond is particularly valuable. This pond with overhanging willows and groups of old thatched cottages, with the Church in the background on the hill, the favourite haunt of the moorhen, was one of the prettiest spots in the village when the sound of the mill-wheel and the pungent smell from the malt-house gave the impression of a more busy life in the now quiet little village. It is also associated with scenes less pleasing and exceedingly unpleasant, when the ducking stool was in use, and the village scold and noisy objectionable females who gave vent to their thoughts in rude language were tied to a chair and dipped in the cool waters of the pond. The village stocks have in many places survived and may be seen. Old oak beams will last for many years, but the ducking stool, or cucking stool as it was called, for which the pond at Ash Priors was famous, has not been preserved. Those who were subjected to this baptism had in some cases to submit to the ordeal of being carried round the parish in the chair and on the following Sunday made to make a public recognition of their offence in church during the time of service, declaring whom they had offended with their tongue and asking them forgiveness after the appointed form.

The fine old 17th century house known as Court House is most attractive and, had it not been modernized, would have been still more so. The name sounds as if it had once been a house where established courts were held. Till quite recently it belonged to the Winters and had no connection with the farm to which it is now attached. It was a private

The Mill Pond, Ash Priors.

house, and at any rate in 1808 it belonged to the Winters and was occupied by Mr. Thomas Winter, who built the stables which have that date upon them and the initials T.W. In some of the rooms there was some fine old oak panelling and mouldings of great beauty round the ceilings, similar to that which may be seen at Sandhill Park, said to be the work of an Italian artist whose work may be found in many parts of Somersetshire, representing grapes and corn and pomegranates. Much, however, of this beautiful work was lost to view by being in a room used as a store-room owing to the windows having been blocked up to avoid the window tax. This fact, however, should give us a clue to the age of the house. The window tax was imposed in 1696 and lasted until 1851. With the exception of very poor cottages, houses with fewer than ten windows paid 2 shillings; those with ten to twenty, 6 shillings; twenty or more, 10 shillings. Accordingly everyone blocked up all the windows they could possibly do without and made themselves ill by living in dark and ill-ventilated rooms.

A fine old painting on a panel in the morning room representing a hunting scene was removed when the property changed hands, but it might as well have been left, as it fell to pieces when it was taken down and could not be put together again.

The house has undergone considerable alterations and improvements from the builders' point of view, in spite of which it still retains some of its ancient glory, when the fine old chestnut tree in the garden, which is kept together by bands and bars, was young. It is, however, a matter of much regret that the quaint old leaden hood which was formerly over the front door was taken down.

Mr. Bryant told me that under that hood there was a beautiful design of the scallop shell. These old leaden hoods are now very rare. I know, however, of one perfect specimen over the entrance of the grand old Manor House, in the street at Collumpton. There, sure enough, is the identical leaden hood with the shell pattern underneath it, without doubt a fac-simile of what was once over the door at Court House. It is said by those who know all about these things that it had no real connection with a shell, but was a derivation from Roman art, where it was used to depict the awning that covered the classic hall or court. The ceilings of tombs were often painted with a representation of this awning, and so the device passed into a pattern for decorative purposes.

During the construction of the farm buildings when this house was converted into a farmhouse, a sad accident occurred. When a wall was being pulled down by means of a chain to which horses were harnessed, Mr. Blackmore had given orders that the work should not be done unless he was there to superintend it. The workmen, however, disregarded the order, and when the horses were about to be started they shouted to one Blanchflower to " look out," who, instead of running away, ran under the wall, which fell upon him, and he was killed.

On a cottage near is a stone let into the south gable with the letters N.B.-W.B., and the date, 1632.

On the coping stone of the corner house, where is the letter box, is the date 1634, with the letters A.P. I have been told that the initials are those of Arthur Periam. If so it would seem to give a clue to the age of Sandhill Park, then called the Hill House, which would date at least as far back as that.

The next house, before it was restored, was the most picturesque in the village, with the steps leading up to it and creeper-clad walls and thatched roof and dormer window. The garden contains the lesser snapdragon (*antirrhinum orontium*). This plant being an annual, the seed must have been imported, and is only found in this garden.

There is no vicarage house at Ash Priors. This appears to be explained by the fact that there are no glebe lands in the parish appropriated to the vicarage upon which to build a house, for the glebe house has for centuries been the creation of successive incumbents who have built or restored it out of their own means or by the system of mortgaging their professional incomes for a term of years. There was an old disused quarry near the Church, probably the one from which the stone was obtained when the Church was built, in which three cottages stood. Sir T. B. Lethbridge had these cottages removed and upon the site built the house known as Rock House, for the incumbent. The Rev. V. C. Day, who occupied it for 48 years, added to the original building a spacious hall and room above it, laid out the garden with much taste and also built a wall round it at his own cost.

There is a well in the garden, it is about 45 feet from the surface to the water which is never more than 18 inches in depth, but fills up as fast as it is drawn out, a beautiful crystal stream issuing from the rock. Near the well is a cistern capable of containing about five hogsheads of water, which is filled by a pump over the well and from thence drawn up into house. The house is occupied by the Vicar so long as he is incumbent of the parish under an agreement with the landlord at a nominal rent, the Vicar being responsible for dilapidations. So that the conditions upon which it is occupied are much the same as an ordinary vicarage, only it is not "the parson's freehold." Growing on the wall you will find the wild Feverfew (*matricaria parthenium*). This is by no means a common wild flower and I thought it a great find when I first discovered it in the neighbourhood. It is said that in every district may be found growing the herb useful as an antidote to the local ailments. When all the land to the south of the parish and the Common were undrained it must have been exceedingly malarious, but at Ash Priors to-day fevers should be few. The plant represents a number of daisy heads on one stem and has a strong aromatic smell and bitter taste, and may easily be mistaken for the garden species.

The village School is a small but useful little building which has served its purpose well for many years. From the windows is a fine view of the Blackdown Hills and the Wellington Monument, standing 900 feet above the level of the sea. This monument was erected by subscription in honour of the Duke of Wellington, who was Lord of the Manor, and in commemoration of his victory at Waterloo. In this undertaking Sir Thomas Lethbridge was chairman of the committee. In this monument he has left a perpetual object lesson in history for the children.

In the schoolroom hangs a board recording the date and purpose for which it was built.

GIVE GOD THE PRAISE.

" This Schoolroom was built at the sole cost and charge of Sir Thomas Buckler Lethbridge, Bart., Anno Domini, 1833; and it was built that the poor children of Ash Priors should be early taught the great truths contained in the Holy Bible and thereby become good Christians and good subjects."

A stone let into the south wall has upon it "Sir T.B.L., A.D. 1833."

The school and the school house belong to Sir Wroth Lethbridge and are let to the managers at a nominal rent of 10 shillings a year. It is under the Somerset County Council, who hold themselves liable for the maintenance of the school provided the parish meet the requirements of the County Education Committee with regard to what is considered adequate accommodation for the children. There are six managers, appointed by the parish under this act in 1903.

In the year 1904 the Education Committee required additional accommodation in the form of a larger play ground, better ventilation and offices. Rather than that it should become a Council School the managers recognised the desirability of trying to raise the moneys. Sir Wroth P. C. Lethbridge undertook to do the work principally at his own expense, thus keeping up the traditions of the family who have always taken so great interest in the parish and all the institutions connected with it.

The following is a list of head teachers since the building of the school in 1833.

Eliza Cridling.
Eliza Stevens.
Mary Ann Stevens.
Sophia Stevens.
Louisa Pullin.
Mrs. Knight, died 1877.
Miss Luck.
Miss Mary Ann Pepper, 1904.
1903 Mrs. Sarah Nicholls.
1904 Mrs. Mary Doble.
1906 Mrs. Mary Jane Newill.

In the year 1870 there were 55 children attending the school. In 1908 there are 20.

A little further up this rugged lane is the West Lodge, another entrance to Sandhill Park, making a short cut across the park to the Church. For the convenience of the family was the little gate at the north-east corner of the Churchyard, which was their special entrance for so many years. That little gate is one of the landmarks which point to the past history of the parish. There is another reason why, though no longer used, it should be retained, and that is that there seems to be a superstition that a churchyard should have two gates. "Did you ever know a churchyard with only one gate?" Another relic of bygone times has just disappeared in the old village pound close to the Church. It had become the receptacle of every old worn out bucket and tin pot and every conceivable thing for which no further use was found, so perhaps it was better that it should disappear, but how much more interesting our country villages would now be if there had been a society for the preservation of old monuments before they were all destroyed. Close to the pound is a small shed which is now used as a place to keep the fuel for the Church stove. This was originally the little stable into which the parson put his horse when he rode over from some neighbouring parish to officiate.

At the corner where you strike the road to Combe Florey is the village inn with the sign of "the Park Gate Inn." It is said to derive its name from its close proximity to the gates of the Highlands, a natural park, a common feature of Somersetshire, where there are many such parks, and which is a part of Sandhill Park. An old house neat and clean, and if you step inside the

landlady will show you with pride the old table in the
bar, which, though at one time a rough board, has from
long use and frequent rubbing with a preparation of her
own making, become quite a handsome piece of furniture,
with as high a polish upon it as some mahogany tables.
It is made of ash. I find the name spelt Island, but
Highland seems to be most appropriate to the situation,
from which such a splendid prospect is obtained of
the surrounding country, and the towers of Bishops
Lydeard, Norton Fitzwarren, Halse, Fitzhead, Kingston,
Bagborough, Cothelstone, and Taunton. Combe Florey,
though so close at hand, is hidden from view. The latter
rectory is noted for having once been held by the Rev.
Sydney Smith, from 1829 till the day of his death, 22nd
February, 1845. The rectory is situated in a deep
wooded glade with park-like surroundings, on one
occasion enhanced by this famous man by a curious
trick played by him upon his friends by fastening stags'
horns to some donkeys, which made an excellent
substitute for the deer.   He wrote describing the
place: "As to wood and lawn, cedar and fir, and pine
and branching palm I have exchanged for the better.
This is a beautiful place with large house and a wood
of three or four acres belonging to it, close to the
house, and a glebe of sixty acres surrounding it, in a
country everywhere most fruitful and fertile.   The
climate, the vegetation and the soil all in strong con-
trast to the north (from which he came) and it well
deserves the name of Combe Florey, for it really is a
valley of flowers, a lovely little spot where nature and
art combine to realize the happy valley." He says " In
those days, *i.e.*, in 1828, the people were poor and
starving." But they were not starving for want of
spiritual food. Their rector is described as of grand

form, powerful countenance, noble and melodious voice.
" In reading the lessons and Psalms he read as almost
to make a commentary on every word, and the meaning
came out so rich and deep.   His sermons were not given
in S. Paul's with more interest and effect, and yet
they were adapted to the congregation from their plain
and practical sense.   In S. Paul's crowded Cathedral
and in the little village church filled with peasantry,
he was always the same." This famous rector was
also a man of inventive mind.   One of his inventions
at least took on, and has survived.   It may be seen
in this parish on the Highlands in the form of the
" Backscratcher."   (See a Memoir of Sydney Smith, by
his daughter.)   Animals have a passion for scratching
their backs.   They break down your gates and palings
to effect this.   The invention was a sharp-edged pole
resting on a high and low post, adapted to every
height from a cow to a lamb.   " You have no idea,"
he says, " how popular it is.   I have not had a gate
broken since I put it up."   The farmer would tell you
it was intended for the animals to rub themselves
against it, but they probably have never heard who
was the inventor of it.

By this road on the other hand you will pass the
Priory, and out again on to the Common.   The old
thatched farmhouse, reflected in the pond, now divided
into three cottages, is known as Ash Farm.   A descendant of a former occupier of this farm speaks of his
father as the parish prentice, by which is meant one
to whom the young boys of the parish were apprenticed
and received into his house, boarded and lodged, and
brought up to the work which they would undertake
when old enough to take service on one of the
farms.

At the famous meeting of occupiers of land in the parish of Ash Priors on 26th July, 1833, referred to later on, "it was further resolved that the ancient custom under the several Acts of Parliament, relating thereto of boarding out the children of the poor, should again be adopted and put into force by the parish officers for the time being."

Thus the youth of the village received their training and better living than they were able to get in their homes, and they became masters in the arts of the various branches of agriculture.

The old farmhouse with two pollard elms at the wicket, thatched roof, and long low window, is a picturesque object from the Common, and a favourite subject of the artist. It was in the barn belonging to this farm that on several occasions of national rejoicing the people of the parish have been entertained at a public dinner. Mrs. Barker alludes to this barn in her letter; she says "there was a grand public dinner held in honour of the Queen's Coronation in a long barn on the Common, with the usual sports afterwards, climbing the greasy pole, and jumping in sacks. All the Lethbridge family came, and every one in the parish, sick or well, had a good feast. We could hear the cannon from Wellington firing the salute. Service first, of course, in Church, and a practical sermon on loyalty."

THE COMMON

THE Common has an historic interest older than the Church or the Priory. It appears to be the remains of what was once the character of the estate of every lord of the manor. A few centuries ago the whole parish was in a sense the common property of the parishioners under the lord of the manor. That is to say, it was like one large farm with many tenants. The land, with the exception of a few home fields or paddocks, was divided into three principal divisions: the arable, the pasture, and the remaining portion of which the soil for certain reasons was not suitable for cultivation, or which lay at a distance and remained uncultivated, which we call " the Common" to-day. The arable portion was let out in lots which were only separated by open strips of grass, called balks (an example of which may still be seen between the Park Gate and Ash Wood) and were thrown open in common as soon as the crops were carried, and remained open until the next sowing, during which time the cattle of the whole community were at liberty to range indiscriminately over the whole field; and so with the meadow land, while the outlying land was grazed in common by the farmers according to the size of their holdings. Thus nearly the whole of the parish was in a sense open land, each person turning out the number of cattle he could feed on his other land in the parish.

All tenants (or renters) had a right to graze their cattle on the open space, and a herdsman for the village was appointed yearly. Every person turning a cow on to the Common had to pay a reasonable sum for the expenses of cleaning out the ditches, and doing other necessary work for the preservation of the Common and towards the wages of the herdsman. The cattle were sent to the herdsman in the morning, whose duty it was to attend at a certain place and to receive into his care the cattle brought to him, and to watch them during the day, and return them to their respective owners in the evening.

As each tenant of the Common fields got permission to enclose his portion of arable and grazing land, the open spaces became gradually smaller and the manor lands became entirely enclosed with the exception only of certain portions for some reasons unsuitable, or not required, of which our Common is an instance, and upon which certain people still have the right to graze their cattle.*

RIGHTS ON THE COMMON.

From the origin of the Common we get at the solution of the question, the vexed question, Who has rights on the Common ?

The persons who had rights on the Common were of two classes: the farmers who held land of the lord of the manor in the Common fields, and the labourers who occupied houses or cottages to which the rights belonged, having been handed down to each succeeding occupier. As long as the system lasted, the actual cultivators of the soil had a voice in settling the

---

*English Village Communities by F. Seebohm, LL.D.

regulations under which the village farm was worked, so that rights on the Common appear to have belonged to persons who cultivated a portion of the arable and meadow land as tenants, or lived in certain houses or cottages which they either owned or rented, to which these rights were attached, and those only who had such a claim possessed rights on the Common.

On Tuesday evening, 19th January, 1904, a meeting was held at the schoolroom for the purpose of testing the opinion of the parishioners as to playing golf on the Common, as a few years ago some little misunderstanding occurred between the villagers and club as to the rights of the Common. Sir Wroth Lethbridge remarked that "four years ago there was a certain amount of talk, he would not say friction, and perhaps misunderstanding as to who held the rights of the Common. He thought the misunderstanding was over estimated. The people who had the rights of the Common were himself, Mr. Savill Onley, Mrs. Winter, Mrs. Blackmore, and Mr. Lockyer, and there were a good many who occupied cottages of his abutting on the Common. He wished them to clearly understand that if he chose to make himself disagreeable and unpleasant, although that was far from his thoughts, he could insist upon his rights to the Common and reserve for himself those rights."

THE COMMON.

The writer of a tourists' guide to Somersetshire in his description of the road between Bishops Lydeard and Milverton, dismisses Ash Priors with the short sentence: "Having crossed an intervening common you take the road to Halse." He could hardly have said less. He might have substituted the

word interesting for intervening, but in these days we
must take into consideration that a cyclist often con-
templates the surface of the road more than the
picturesque surroundings, more especially when toiling
against the strong westerly wind which usually meets
you when crossing the dead level of the exposed bit
of road which runs across the Common.

> Here when aurora first begins to dawn
> The wakeful lark springs mounting from the lawn,
> Poised by their plumes in lofty flights they play,
> With joyful warblings hail th' approaching day,
> But when the sun displays a purple scene,
> And drinks the pearly dew, that decked the green,
> A thousand tuneful birds in concert meet,
> A thousand tuneful notes the groves repeat,
> And when their music ceases with the day,
> Sweet Philomel chants her pensive lay.*

The Common has a flora and a fauna of its own.
In spring at the end of March may be found a little
plant which frequents moist pastures and swampy
heaths, called the lesser red rattle (*pedicularis sylvatica*).
It is also known by the less pretty name, louse wort,
from the belief that sheep eating it become diseased
and covered with parasites.

This evil is due rather to the fact of the sheep
being allowed to graze in the moist pastures, and so
far from attaching any blame to the plant its presence
should be a warning to the farmer to pay attention to
the drainage of the locality where it grows. From
the Common you may get a view of Sandhill Park,
the noble mansion which takes its name from the site
on which it stands. This view from the western end
of the Common was described to me as one of the

* The nightingale may be heard on the Common.

prettiest views in West Somerset. The house is said
to date from the beginning of the 18th century; an old
painting which hangs on the walls on the staircase
represents it as a small red stone residence surrounded
by a wall, a ploughman with two yoke of oxen ploughing almost up to the gates. It stands now in an
open park upon a warm dry sandy hill enjoying the
mild climate of the district, a sunny aspect and a
glorious prospect; a country seat more charmingly
situated it would be difficult to find, one of the advantages of the long approaches to it being that it combines
seclusion without obstruction.

In summer from the arched bramble a restless
noisy little bird all day continally utters the quick
chat chat that has suggested the name that it commonly goes by. Here, too, you may see the horned
sheep grazing, and at Michaelmas, or at least before,
a flock of cackling geese at the pond. The flicker of
a fire under the hedge and the curling smoke indicate
the gipsy's encampment, the usual complement of the
Common. Few who pass over it fail to remark its beauty.
If the village of Ash Priors is not well known, anyone will
direct you to Ash Common. Covered for the most part
with gorse, in summer may be seen here and there
bright patches of purple heath or ling (*caluna vulgaris*).
This is not the plant from which the bees get the
honey. They have to go farther afield for that, probably as far as the Quantocks, which are covered with
heather (*erica cinerea*), and cross-leaved heath (*erica
tetralis*) as well as ling, and which yield the dark
thick heather honey which the bees of Ash Priors
bring home in the autumn. Here, too, in autumn the
botanist will find the curious little plant known as
lady's tresses (*neottia spiralis*), with tuberous root and

flowers which are arranged in a single row, and in spiral manner, in some specimens from left to right, in others from right to left, round the upper portion of the stalk. The flowers are said to be fragrant in the evening.

It is also said of this little plant, and I believe it to be true, that it is very uncertain in its appearance, and that you cannot depend upon finding a single plant the next summer on a spot where thousands were to be found the previous year. The furze has suffered terribly during the last few years, partly from clearings made for drives on that portion which was marked out for the golf course, but also by fires lit to commemorate the 5th November, by which the furze has been destroyed and no good end gained.

Goldsmith describes it as "unprofitably gay," but it is by no means "unprofitable," although it may be "gay." In former days when bread was baked at home, the poor would be fully alive to the value of furze faggots, than which few things give a greater heat when burnt in the oven. The tender young shoots were quite recently used as fodder for the cattle, and the ashes yielded a valuable dressing for the land. In one cottage there is a very small room not much larger than a cupboard. The occupant of the house told me that it was once a farm house, and that little room was used for storing wood ashes, which before artificial preparations came into use, were mixed by the farmer with the seed when sowing turnips. In these days when neither the tender shoots nor wood ashes are used, and bread is no longer baked at home, the faggots are not in demand. If we have no further use for it in our time, we may well forbear to destroy a plant which if allowed to grow adds so much to the beauty of the Common. It is told of Linnæus, the famous Swedish botanist, that when he came to England and for the first time beheld the furze, he fell down on his knees and thanked God for having made so beautiful a plant.

The harvest of the Common is in the autumn, when the blackberry pickers come out in shoals to gather quite a rich harvest, as may be seen at the railway station, in the astonishing quantity of fruit which is sent off for the London market for blackberry tarts and jam, and for another purpose for which they are equally in demand, to be made into dye. And when the blackberry picking has brought the labours of the year to a close, and the purple heath has yielded to the russet brown of withering brake and bramble, and the furze is bursting out again into its autumn bloom,

> The nimble stag skims o'er th' unbending grass;
> The way which fear directs he trembling tries;
> Nor knows where fear directs, or where he flies.
> A hundred different sounds assail his ears,
> A death in every different sound he fears.
> And now he faintly moves a slower pace;
> And closer now the hounds pursue the chase,
> Till in despair back on his foes he turns,
> Makes feeble efforts with his branchy horns;
> Short is the combat, soon he yields his breath,
> And gasping falls, and trembling pants in death.

I have in my mind one November afternoon catching a glimpse of the scarlet coats of the huntsmen returning from the chase and, hearing the note of the horn as they crossed the Common as the sun was sinking red behind a forest of trees in the west,

recalling Keble's beautiful lines for the 23rd Sunday
after Trinity :—

> Red o'er the forest peers the setting sun,
> The line of yellow light dies fast away
> That crowned the eastern copse ; and chill and dun
> Falls on the moor the brief November day.
>
> .   .   .   .
>
> Now the tired hunter winds a parting note,
> And echo bids good night from every glade.

But who knows the story of the Common ?—the
open common, about which nevertheless there seems
to hang a veil of mystery. Who lit the fires which
burnt the gorse ? Who drove their carts across it
and spoilt the turf ? Who wrecked the pavilion built
by Major Wise when the first golf links were made ?
What became of the book ? No one knows. We
know that Betsy Isaacs was delivered of a still-born
child on Ash Common on the night of the 12th October,
1902, and that Mr. Seaward was thrown out of
his cart whilst attempting to cross the Common on
the dark night of the 8th March, 1905, lay there until
the morning, and died in his daughter's arms. We
know that many a bell was cast on Ash Common by
the famous bellanter, Roger Semson, which has rung
in many a wedding peal ; but where the foundry was
no one knows.

Who knows where the plover makes her nest, with no
attempt at concealment, on the open spaces of the
Common ? Who knows where the night jar, heard in
summer evenings on the Common, lays her eggs with
no nest at all ? Or the nightingales ?

> Where the thickest boughs are twining
> Of the greenest, darkest tree,
> There they plunge the light declining,
> All may hear but none may see.

ASH PRIORY

SOMEWHERE about the year 1115, William Giffard, Bishop of Winchester (for the manor of Taunton belonged to the Bishops of Winchester), founded in that town and endowed a priory of canons regular of the order of S. Augustine.

Except for certain references to the property of the Priors of Taunton at Ash, the Reeve's account, and the traces of the buildings which still remain, the authority we have for the belief there was once a religious house in Ash Priors is the bare statement in Mr. Collinson's *History of Somerset* that "the Priors of Taunton had a house at Ash Priors, the ruins of which were taken down about the year 1784."

The question which we have to decide, after weighing the evidence available, is whether it was a sub-priory or only a manor house, the residence of the lord's bailiff? Anyway the existence of this house and the fact that the priors of Taunton were lords of the manor of Ash gave to Ash the additional name of Priors, or as it is said, to distinguish it from another manor in the same parish called Ash Herberts. But as no Herbert seems to have had lands in Ash Priors between 1280 and 1428, and there is no mention of Ash Herbert in the *Feudal Aids* between those dates, Ash Priors was probably so called to distinguish it from Ash in Martock, also spelt Esse, and Ashbrittle, spelt Esse Brittel.

The only light I have discovered with reference to Ash Herberts is from the will of Thomas Selwoode, of Ash Priors, Somerset, gent., dated 8th April, 1571. Thomas Selwoode is lord of the manor of Ash Priors by conveyance from Christopher Stevens who had it on a lease from Sir John Leigh, knight, of London. By this will Thomas Selwoode bequeathed the issues and profits of his lands called "Asharberts" in Bishops Lydeard to William Norris and Roger Grevis on the renunciation of Johan the relict. His wife Jone executrix (*Somerset Wills*, Vol. III., page 63).

The Priory of Taunton soon after its foundation became a wealthy and flourishing community. In the reign of Henry II. the canons obtained a charter of confirmation of grants made to them by several benefactors from their founder downwards, among which appears :—

"Ex dono Roberti Arundelli, duas hidas terræ apud Aissam et ecclesiam ejusdem villæ cum pertinentiis suis."

In the year 1288 Pope Nicholas IX. granted the tenths of all ecclesiastical benefices which, together with the first fruits, had for a long time been paid to the Roman See, to King Ed. I. for six years as a means of defraying the cost of a crusade, and according to the taxation made for this purpose the Priory of Taunton is said to be possessed of lands in Esse Prioris valued at eight shillings. In a charter granted in the reign of King Edward III., dated 1st October, 1334, in a long list of donations which show the Priory to have been one of the wealthiest in the country, Ash Priors appears more than once. In addition to the original gift of two hides of land by Robert Arundell, there was the gift of Robert Ferown of land in Esshe;

the gift of Gilbert de Thorne of one ferling of land in Esse ; the gift of Maurice de Legge of five acres of land in Esse ; the gift of Jordan de Molton of the land of Pyleigh with all its appurtenances.

The Rectory of Ash Priors was one of those which was appropriated to the Priory, *i.e.*, they owned the tithes and had spiritual charge of the parish, and were responsible for the services in the Church. Whether these duties were performed by one of the canons riding out from Taunton, with an annual allow- ance of two shillings for shoeing his horse, or whether John Sealake, who received a salary of 113 shillings and fourpence as chaplain of Esse was resident in the " house " in the parish, or one of the secular clergy from a neighbouring parish did the work, has never been explained.

The Black Canons of Aissa had as neighbours the Knights Hospitallers and the Knights Templars at Stalford, in Halse, but they do not appear to have lived on very friendly terms. Soon after their acquisi- tion of the manor of Halse they institute a law suit against the Prior of Taunton in the year 1275, on the feast of S. Martin. The Assize is held at Montacute in the fourth year of Edw. I's reign, and the Hos- pitallers are awarded a decree in their favour in the matter of an attempt on the part of the Prior of Taunton to narrow a road in Esse so as to render it impassible for a vehicle, and thus to the injury of the free tenement of the Hospitallers in Halse.

Though covering a much larger area than the pre- sent house and buildings the Priory would not be a very large one. There is a date (1529) in the left spandrel of the arch over the porch. Whether that is the date of the old house or of a later addition to

The Priory.

it, it could not have had a very long existence when
we remember that the monasteries were dissolved in
1539. The present house cannot be supposed to be
as old as that, although it may be very much older
than it looks from the outside. The house has certainly undergone many alterations in the process of
adapting it to modern ideas of comfort and health.
The verandah and large windows have entirely altered
the character of the house, the windows originally
being in keeping with the Tudor arch of the porch,
i.e., divided by heavy stone mullions into larger portions at the bottom and smaller at the top. When
we say that not one stone of the original buildings is
left standing upon another, it must not be taken
literally, for upon closer inspection it appears that the
old walls were adapted to the requirements of a
modern house, some of the walls being five feet thick.
In the back part of the house, where there is clearly
evidence of a circular stair and also of a conversion
of the old into the new, there is a remarkable thickness
of wall about eight feet square, suggesting the position
of a secret chamber, and the long passages suggest dor-
mitories now divided up into rooms and a passage.

With a great block of masonry thus unaccounted
for in the centre of the house which has always been
known as the Priory, it is not surprising that strange
noises which cannot be accounted for should be associated with that thickness of the wall.

There is also another semi-circular depression in the
wall of the staircase which once formed part of a turret
stair, and which has been ingeniously converted into
an alcove filled with beautiful things.

Some of the foundations of the old buildings were
discovered when improvements were being made in the

garden by the present owner. The people of Taunton
have little less clue to the plan of the mother Priory
than we of Ash Priors have of our own. Even during
the process of putting in deep sewers, laying gas and
water mains and excavations for foundations of houses
upon what is known as the site of the Priory in that
town not a bit of solid wall was found, but there was
abundant evidence that buildings existed there from the
great quantity of rubble, mortar and broken stones
which turned up everywhere. It would seem that the
place had been used as a quarry to get stone for
building elsewhere, so that there was nothing left to
tell the tale of its former magnificence. The same no
doubt took place at Ash Priors, and it may reasonably
be supposed that much of the stone which formed part
of the ruins of the old buildings was used for building
the present house, and worked into walls and cottages,
perhaps some of which are now standing.

In 1536 an act for the dissolution of the smaller
houses to the number of 376 was passed by Parliament.
In 1539 an act was passed regulating the voluntary
surrender of the larger ones. William Williams was
the last Prior of Taunton, who with 12 canons met in the
Chapter House on the 12th Feb., 1539, and in the presence
of the Commissioner, John Tregonwell, unwillingly
signed the instrument of surrender, and so for the second
time the Manor and Rectory of Ash Priors was taken
away from the Church and has never been restored.

Those who would know the history of Taunton
Priory should get the learned work on the subject by
Mr. Thomas Hugo and read in his elegant language
the result of his labours amongst "Stores examined
and collected from many a ponderous volume, thickly
written roll and faded charter." But, strange to say,

though he mentions Esse so often in his account, he never once mentions the Priory, not even under the name of a manor or court house, or even " a house." Now as it is an undoubted fact that the Priors of Taunton had a house at Ash, from which the place obtained the additional name of Esse Prioris or Ash Priors, we should have looked to him to throw some light upon a subject about which we desire to know more.

When Commissioners were appointed by Parliament to enquire into and report upon the value of all ecclesiastical possessions throughout the country, the returns which were made by these officers known as the "Valor Ecclesiasticus," furnishes us with a complete account of the possessions of the Priory of Taunton immediately before the suppression. It shows also what sums were paid to clerical and lay persons, and the amount spent in alms.

HOUSE AND PRIORY OF TAUNTON.

Declaration of the extent and annual value of all and singular the lands and tenements and other possessions with the tithes, oblations, and all other issues of the divers benefices and chapels belonging and appropriated to the aforesaid Priory, in the time of William Andrewes, now Prior thereof.

ESSE (Ash Priors).

Value in assized rents of the customary tenants	vii	iii	ix.
Demesne lands	x	iii	ii.
Out of this a rent annually to William Francis		vii	o
Do. To the Lord of the Manor of Bishops Lydearde		xii	o
Perquisites of the courts		xxx	o
Fines of lands		xliii	o

Amongst the issues and profits of the tithes of grain, with other tithes and casualties of chapels, are :—

Tithes of grain of Esse with the oblations
and other casualties ...   ...   vii xiii v.

From items to be deducted under the heading, allowances, pensions and stipends :

To John Sealake, Chaplain of Esse ...   cxiii^s : iiii^d·

The tithes are given as £110 imp. There can be little doubt that originally tithes might be paid at the discretion of the donor to whom he would; but as parishes came to be formed, a parishioner would, in his own interests, devote the tithes to the priest of his own parish and the Bishop would stand out for such a permanent possession before consenting to consecrate a church.

While the monastic system prevailed in England it was open to the patron of a living to appropriate the Rectory to a monastery; thereupon the obligation devolved on the monastic body to provide for the spiritual service of the parish church, which it did by appointing a vicar or deputy. It resulted in the monastery taking what are called the Rectorial Tithes on corn, hay, wood, and leaving to the vicar the small tithes which came from the less important produce of the land. In this way, at the dissolution of the monasteries in the reign of Henry VIII, about one fourth of the whole amount of tithe passed into the hands of the great laity on whom church lands were lavished by the king, or to the Colleges at the Universities, which were endowed with monastic revenues.*

---

* This is precisely what happened at Ash Priors, and hence the alienation of the tithes from the benefice, which are called Impropriated, i.e., placing the tithes in the hands of a layman, the impropriety of which is obvious.

In order to facilitate the disposal of the estates after the dissolution, a new survey and valuation were taken, usually called " the Ministers' accounts," which were compiled from the foregoing survey and other similar returns.

THE LATE PRIORY OF TAUNTON, SOMERSET.

ESSE.

	£	s.	d.
Rents of the free tenants		xx	o
Assized rents	xvj	vj	viij
Farm of the Manor and Rectory ...		xlvj	ix
Perquisites of the Court		viij	v^{ob}

At the dissolution of the monasteries, Henry VIII. granted the manor and rectory of Ash Priors to John Leigh as is shown in the following reference to Esse in 1556 from the Land Revenue Records at the Public Record Office.

" In the third year of Edward VI, . . supreme head on earth of the church of England and Ireland, among the lands and possessions of the late Priory of Taunton was Maund. de Esse cum Rectoria ibm, from which were received xlvi^{s.} viij^{d.} for annual rent or one-tenth part of the whole manor with Rectory, these in the letters patent of the late King Henry VIII, given under his great seal of England the 16th day of January, the 35th year of the reign of his Majesty, to John Leigh, his heirs and assignees for ever granted reserving the said annual rent to the lord king and his successors. And the said annual rent of one-tenth is accounted for in the account of John Aylworth, Esquire, Receiver of the lord the King of the Court of Augmentation in the county of Somerset."

From John Leigh this tenth part of the manor came to Sir John Leigh. We next find Thomas

Selwood, of Ash Priors, lord of the manor, who had it by conveyance from Christopher Stephens, to whom it had been leased by Sir John Leigh. At the expiry of the lease it would revert to Sir John Leigh or his heirs. His daughter Agnes was his heir, and she married Edward Fitzgarrat. The Fitzgarrats joined in conveying the manor to John More and John Bostock. Somewhere about this time, in 1616, part of the manor of Ash Priors is bequeathed by Nicholas Streate, of Bridgwater, to his second son Edward Streate. It must have been a portion of the manor only which in 1548 was possessed by Bishop Barlow, who is said to have exchanged it with Edward VI for other lands. Eventually I find in 1723, Hugh Bickham bequeathing the manor and rectory of Ash Priors to his eldest son, Hugh, and John Lethbridge inheriting it through his marriage with the daughter of John Periam.

Thus, roughly, we have the names of the lords of the manor and lay rectors of Ash Priors, which should be traced in two lines, from the time when they were conferred upon Asser by King Alfred, after whose death they were held by the Bishops of Sumersætan or of Wells, from the time of Bishop Athelm in 909 to that of Bishop Giso in 1061, and so on.

1063. Harold, Earl of Kent.
Roger de Arundel.
Robert de Arundel.
The Priors of Taunton.

1539. John Leigh (a tenth part).
Sir John Leigh.

1548. William Barlow, Bp. of Bath and Wells.
Christopher Stephens.

1571. Thomas Selwood.
       Agnes Fitzgarrat.
       John More and John Bostock.
       Nicholas Streate.
1616. Edward Streate.
       Hugh Bickham.
1723. Hugh Bickham.
       John Periam.
1755. John Lethbridge.

An historic interest attaches to Bishop Barlow, he being one of the four bishops who took part in the consecration of Archbishop Parker, a detailed account of which is contained in the register of Lambeth.

When under Queen Mary the kingdom returned to the Roman allegiance, Papal Bishops were intruded into some of the Sees, their lawful holders being ejected, There was consequently some danger of the episcopal succession in England being broken, when Elizabeth came to the throne. The idle tale put forth by the Romanists, which for a time obtained some credence, was that the consecration of Archbishop Parker was irregular, being performed by incompetent persons at the Nag's Head Tavern in Cheapside, which if true would invalidate the orders of those bishops who received consecration through him.

Copy of the Will of Hugh Bickham, Esqre., among the wills of Somerset, now deposited in Somerset House, an abstract of which was made by the late Rev. Frederick Brown :—

Hugh Bickham, of Taunton St. James, Somerset, Esqre., will dated 22 June, 1723-4, proved Feb. 22, 1723-4 by Rachel, the relict and Hugh Bickham the son [23 Bolton]. My eldest daughter Elizabeth, wife of Mr. Thomas Cross, is, for I provided sufficiently for her on her marriage with Paulet Asterley, Gent., her former husband, decd. My daughter Bridget, wife of Mr. Nicholas Hare, an annuity of £20. Rachel, now my wife. To my youngest son, John Bickham, £800 at age of 24. To my eldest son, Hugh Bickham, the manor and rectory of Ash Priors, Somerset, lands in West Monkton, etc., Somerset, Messuages in Hambrook, Stapleton, etc., co. Glouc."

Those who maintain that there was never a Priory at Ash Priors, but only a house—a sort of summer residence—where the Prior of Taunton spent a few months in the year, or merely a residence of the steward who looked after the property belonging to the Priory of Taunton in this parish, answering to the description given of it by Mr. Collinson as a court or manor house, are probably speaking without authority, and making the mistake of using the word " house" in its conventional instead of its technical sense, as meaning a religious establishment. I am much more inclined to think that it answered rather to the description of the small house of White Friars, founded by Walter de Meriet, lord of the manor of Combe Florey, the site of which was in that part of the parish of Bishops Hull which adjoins Taunton. The old house which stood on this spot and which (like the Priory at Ash Priors) has been rebuilt, was known by the name of Paul's Abbey.

It is supposed that this house had been suppressed or dissolved before the general dissolution of the monasteries, which also may have been the case at Ash Priors, and help to clear up the difficulty of the date on the porch.

There was also another small monastery or priory of canons regular of S. Augustine at Stavordale in the county of Somerset, which was united to the Priory of Taunton. This house found a chaplain to say divine service every day in the Priory Church of Stavordale, and to pray for the soul of the founder. This priory is now converted into a farm house and barn. There are remains of ecclesiastical architecture in that barn which point to its having been the chapel, two good gothic arches. Now the only bits of ecclesiastical architecture which we can point to in our Priory from which to read a page of its history, are its porch and a little bit of quadrifoil moulding in a stone let into the gable of the barn, but not sufficient to give the idea that the barn was ever a chapel.

If my researches have failed to convince any one that there was ever what we should understand by a Priory at Ash Priors, the fact that the house has always been known as "The Priory," and the evidence furnished by the substantial structure which still stands on the site of the old buildings, the discovery of more extensive foundations lead me to the conclusion that the house which belonged to the Priors of Taunton in this parish was of considerable size and importance, and an establishment belonging to a religious order would certainly be conducted in a manner becoming the order to which it belonged.

Had the suppression of the monasteries not come and put an end to its existence, the recent addition to the buildings (which the date on the porch suggests) leads to the conclusion that it was in process of development, and was no doubt intended to supply the needs of the poor of the district.

A familiar sight in Ash Priors in those days in the lanes would be a monk, breviary in hand. The canons of this order are said to have occupied a half-way position beween monks and secular clergy. He wore an alb which reached to the feet, and was fastened round his waist by a girdle of black leather. His amice enwrapped his shoulders like a cloak, over these he had a long black mantle to which was fastened a hood of the same colour, and a high black cap covered his head.

They lived a hardy regular life rather than one of privations. The worst they had to contend with would be the cold of the bare dormitory and the wind-swept cloister where the monks spent so much of their time, but this was not the experience of monks alone in those days. They were warmly clothed and lived well. Their habits, though of coarse material, were made of wool and closely woven. Their food, though plain, was of the best home made bread, made from pure wheat flour, from their own mill probably, the old mill which is still standing; the best of milk and butter from the Manor Farm, and home-brewed ale.

Daily Life at the Priory.

The monks rose early, between five and six, washed on the cold stones of the open lavatory, then took their places in the chapel at six of the clock. There they said matins and prime and heard the Mass. Then came breakfast, followed by terce, after which they dispersed for the temporal business of the day which in a self-supporting establishment would provide plenty of occupation for everybody. Some taught or learned in the draughty cloister. Some did the ordinary work of the house. Some attended the sick in the hospital. Some attended to the stores, grinding the flour at the mill, brewing the ale, baking the bread, dispensing the food, and preparing the meals. Whilst the lay brethren went forth to the Priory fields to superintend the work of the farm or to work with their own hands, and attend to the cattle, all except those otherwise detained, would be expected to assemble in chapel for sixt and nones at noon and at three o'clock, and at the mid-day meal in the refectory eating in silence, while some one from a little pulpit in the wall would read to them passages from the lives of the saints. Then

> "Be the day weary or be the day long,
> At length it ringeth to evensong."

Then followed the evening meal in the refectory, and in the winter evenings they might sit round the great wood fire on the hearth and warm themselves until the curfew bell from the church tower bade them rake out the fire and retire to rest in the long dormitory above, by the turret staircase, to be awaked in the morning by the sound of the Priory bell, which has been ringing ever since the 12th century, save only for the interval which elapsed between the pulling down of the old buildings, and the building of the present house.

Compotus of lands belonging to Taunton Priory in the parish of Esse, 1438-9.

Brit. Mus. Abb. Roll, 25,873.

Esse

Compotus Johannis atte Water prepositi ibidem de anno quo infra Regis Henrici sexti septimo decimo.

frumentum

Et de quinque quarteriis frumenti retornati de exitu bladorum pervenientium de decimis bladorum ibidem hoc anno tritorum pro stramine ad usum hospicii ibidem et non plus quia residuum venditur in grosso ut patet in venditione bladorum, &c.

Summa v quarteria.

Siligo

De quibus compotum liberat prioratui Taunton ut pro pencione capellani de Esse hoc anno iii quarteria frumenti item liberat dicto prioratui ut pro pencione ballivi domini ii quarteria frumenti.

Summa quia supra   ...   et eque [æque].

Et de iiii bussellis siliginis retornati de exitu decime arum garbarum ibidem hoc anno tritarum pro stramine ut supra et residuum venditur in grosso ut patet.

Summa iiii bussella,

De quibus compotum liberat prioratui ut pro pencione capellani de Esse hoc anno iiii bussella siliginis.

Summa quia supra   ...   et eque [æque].

De decimis garbarum residuum nihil hic quia venditur in grosso ut patet in venditione decimarum, etc.

Arreragia   Et de x^s i^d obolo [$\frac{1}{2}$d.] de arreragiis suis anni precedentis

Summa x^s i^d obol.

Redditum assise.   Et de xxxviii^s $x\frac{1}{4}^d$ de toto redditu assise ibidem cum firma molendini termini Nativitatis domini et de xliv^s xi^d de eodem redditu termini Pasche. Et de xxxix^s $vi\frac{1}{4}^d$ & de eodem redditu termini Nativitatis S. Johannis Baptiste. Et xlvii^s ii^d obol de eodem redditu termini Michaelis. Et de iiii^d de redditu de Wodelond. Et de ix^{li} xviii^s xi^d obol de toto redditu terre dominicalis dimisse diversis tenentibus domini ut patet in rotulo computi anno regni Ricardi nuper regis Anglie xxii^{de} et de ii^d de novo redditu nuper Ricardi Deigher pro uno messuagio in australi parte molendini domini nunc in manu Johannis Torre.

Summa xviii^{li} xi^s x^d obol.

Venditio tolcorn et feni.   De iii bussellis de tolcorn provenientibus de decima molendini de Cotheleston [Cothelstone] de certo annuatim unde i bussellum frumenti i bussellum siliginis et i bussellum ordii. Et venditionem [?cancelled] hoc anno liberat prioratui. Et de x^d obol. de decima feni de pitpathe hoc anno venditi.

Summa x^d obol.

Perquisita curie cum . . . et heriett.   Et de xx^d de perquisitis curie legalis termini Michaelis ut patet in eadem. Et de iii^s iiii^d de pannagio porcorum ut patet in eadem. Et de xiii^s iiii^d de fine Johannis Torre pro illo cotagio scito in vico erga molendinum domini quod Ricardus Deigher pretenuit Tenendum eidem Johanni ut patet in eadem

curia. Et de vi^d de herietto Ricardi Deigher pro
successione dicti cotagii ut patet in eadem curia.
Et de vi^d de herietto Johannis Glagge pro sursumred
ditione unius cotagii cum ii acris terre incluse et i
acra terre apud le Dowen ut patet in eadem curia.
Et de viii^s iiii^d de fine Willelmi Freman pro illo cotagio
cum predictis iii acris terre quod dictus Johannes
Glagge pretenuit Tenendum eidem Will. Freman ut
patet in eadem curia. Et de v^s i^d de perquisitis curie
legali termini Hock ut patet in eadem. Et de xiii^d de
perquisitis curie tente die Veneris proximo ante festum
Nativitatis S. Johannis Baptiste ut patet in eadem.
Et de xl^s de fine Roberti atte Wille pro reversione
illius tenementi cum pertinentiis quod Johannes Paull
senior pretenuit. Tenendum eidem Roberto Wille ut
patet in eadem curia et de v^s de fine Ricardi Deigher
pro reversione illius messuagii cum curtilagio et iii
acris terre quod Ibeta Menbury modo tenet Tenendum eidem Ricardo ut patet in eadem curia. Et de
xxxvi^s viii^d de fine Johannis Mount senioris illius terre
et pasture in boxo domini de *Esse* quod Johannes
Paull senior modo tenet. Tenendum eidem Johanni
Mount ut patet in eadem curia. Et de vi^d de fine
Baldewini Beram ut morare possit extra dominium ut
patet in eadem curia.

Summa cxvi^s.

Summa totalis recepta cum arreragiis
xxiiii^li xviii^s x^d obol.

**Defectus
redditus** Idem computus in defectu redditus molendinii per
annum ix^s. In defectu redditus molendinii per annum
ix^s. In defectu redditus Thome Person prius
Nicholai Fursy pro terra dominicali per annum x^s v^d.
In defectu redditus terre dominicalis in le Sterte que
solebant reddere per annum xxvii^s et modo de tanto
ad minorem redditum per annum vii^s.

Summa xxvi^s v^d.

Idem computat in expensis senescalli celerarii et
aliorum supervenientium ad curiam legalem termino
Hock v^s vi^d in expenso senescalli ad curiam termino
Nativitatis S Johannis Baptiste iiii^d in expenso senes-

calli celerarii ad curiam legalem termino Michaelis in anno sequenti Regis Henrici Nunc xviii^{imo} iiii^a iii^d ob. Item in victualibus cervisia et candelis de Johanne Torre pro domino priore apud *Esse* existente ut patebat pro uno tallagio inter eos facto vi^a viii^d· Item liberat fabrice ecclesie de Esse ad turrim campanarum ibidem ex dono domini prioris vi^a viii^d· Item solutis Thome Deygher ad careandum decimas bladorum de Esse usque grangiam in autumno ad thoxam vi^L Item solutos Johanni atte Water pro raylyng et dawbyng circa novam grangiam ad thravam ii^a Item solutos eidem Johanni atte Water conducto per x dies adiuvantibus lathamis et aliis operariis circa dictam novam grangiam tam pro die cum mense ii^d xx^d· Item in i quarterio calcis eidem grangie empto ix^d· Item in Crestes pro nova grangia de *Esse* emptis xxi^d· In i ulage pro consemili empto ii^d· Item solutos Johanni atte Watere pro focali prosternendo et aliis iutis et husbandriis hoc anno ibidem per ipsum factis ut constat per i billam ii^s v^d obol. Item solutos Ricardo Deigher ad thaxam pro area in nova grangia facienda xii^d· Item solutos Ricardo Deigher pro sternendo focali per vices anni ad thaxam ut constat per i billam ii^s viii^d· Item solutos Thome Deigher carianti fenum decime parochie usque curiam ad thaxam ii^d· Item eidem Thome carianti focali de Aysshewode usque curiam iii^d· Item solutos Johanni Paull juniori per genti novam grangiam de Rubbage ibidem iii^L Item predictus Johannes atte Watere petit allocatum pro i billa de diversis materiis et domus tegulanda et focali prosternendo ut patet pro dicta billa et allocantur viii^s iii^d·

Summa l^s ix^d·

Solutio foris. Item computat solutos domino de Comb Flury de certo redditu per annum vii^L Item solutos ecclesie de Lydeard Episcopi pro denaris S. Petri iiii^d· Item collectum curie de hundrede de Lydeard episcopi pro secta ibidem per annum ii^L

Summa ix^s iiii^d·

Liberat
denarios.

Idem computum liberat domino priori de redditu etallis proficius hoc anno per i tallea   ix^{li} viii^s iiii^d·
Item liberat domino Joh. Gay capellano de Esse hoc anno pro pencione sua .   .   .   .   c^s·
Et liberat domino priori de fine Willelmi Freman per manus competentes .   .   .   .   viii^s iiii^d·
Et eidem domino priori super auditum computi per manus competentes .   .   .   xii^s
Et eidem domino de fine Joh. Munt senioris per manus eius . . . . . . xxxvi^s viii^d·
Et eidem domino de fine Roberti atte Wille per manus eius . . . . . . vi^s viii^d·
                  Summa xvii^{li} xii^s·
Summa omnium misericordiarum liberacionum et solucionum .   .   .   . xxi^{li} xviii^s vi^d·
Et sic debentur domino .   .   .   lx^s iiii^d ob.
De quibus allocantur eidem .   .   .   ii^s vii^d·
Soluti domino super auditum computi. Et allocantur eidem vi^d soluti Ricardo Deigher pro focali in boxo domini prostrato per vices condonato super auditum compoti. Et allocantur eidem iii^s i^d ob. pro bono servicio euisdem compoti hoc anno et anno elapso facto. Et allocantur eidem iii^s iiii^d de amerciamento Walteri Mounte condonati per dominum super auditum compoti. Et allocantur eidem compoto x^s soluti domino priori post presentem compotum in festo concepcionis beate Marie virginis.
           Summa allocationum xix^s vi^d ob.
        Et sic nunc debent domino xl^s x^d·

Unde
super

Robertum atte Wille de fine suo aretro xxxiii^s iiii^d·
Baldewinum Beram de antiquis arreragiis suis vii^s vi^d·

Translation of the foregoing.

Esse.

    Account of John atte Water reeve there for the 17th year of King Henry VIth (1439).

Corn.

    And of five quarters of corn retained from the issues of corn coming from the tithes of corn there thrashed this year for straw for the use of the inn there and not more because the residue is sold in gross as appears in the sale of corn.
                  Total 5 quarters.

Of which the accountant delivers to the Priory of Taunton as for the pension of the chaplain of Esse this year three quarters of corn. He delivers two quarters of corn to the said Priory as for the pension of the lord's bailiff, 2 quarters of corn.

Total because above and equally.

Siligo.

And of four bushels of siligo retained from the issues of the tithes of sheaves there this year thrashed for straw as above and the residue is sold in gross as appears, etc.

Total 4 bushels.

Of which the accountant delivers to the Priory as for the pension of the chaplain of Esse this year four bushels of siligo. Total as above and equally.

Of the tithes of sheaves there is no residue here because it is sold in gross as appears in the sale of tithes, etc.

Arrears.

And of 10s. 1½d. of his arrears of the preceding year.

Total 10s. 1½d.

Rent ot Assize.

And of 38s. 9¼d. of the total rent of assize there with the ferm of the mill for the term of Christmas. And of 46s. 11d. of the same rent for the term ot Easter. And of 39s. 6¼d. of the same rent for the term of the Nativity of St. John the Baptist. And of 47s. 2½d. of the same rent for the term of Michaelmas. And 4d. from the rent of Wodelond. And £9 18s. 11½d. from the entire rent of the demesne land from divers tenants of the lord as appears in the roll of the account for the 22nd year of the reign of Richard lately King of England. And of 2d. of new rent lately Richard Deighers for a messuage in the southern part of the mill of the lord now in the hand of John Torre.

Total £18 11s. 10½d.

Sale of Tolcorn and Hay.

Of three bushels of tolcorn coming from the tithe of the mill of Cotheleston "de cárto" annually whereof one bushel of corn one bushel of siligo and one bushel of barley. And he delivers it this year to the Priory. And of 10½d. of the tithe of hay of Pitpathe sold this year.

Total 10½d.

**Perqui-
sites of
the Court
with . . .
and
Heriots.**

And of 2od. of perquisites of the law court for the term of Michaelmas as appears in the same. And of 3s. 4d of pannage of pigs as appears in the same. And 13s. 4d. from the fine of John Torre for that cottage situated in the street towards the lord's mill which Richard Deigher held before to Hold to the same John as appears in the same Court. And 6d. from the heriot of Richard Deigher for the succession of the said cottage as appears in the same Court. And 6d. from the heriot of John Glagge for the surrender of a cottage with two acres of land enclosed and one acre of land at the Dower as appears in the same Court. And 8s. 4d. from the fine of William Freman for that cottage with the aforesaid three acres of land which the said John Glagge held before to Hold to the same William Freman as appears in the same Court. And of 5s. 1d. from perquisites of the Law Court for the term of Hock as appears in the same. And of 13d. from the perquisites of the Court held on the Friday next before the Feast of the Nativity of St. John the Baptist as appears in the same. And of 40s. from the fine of Robert atte Wille for the reversion of that tenement with appurtenances which John Paull senior held before to hold to the same Robert Wille as appears in the same Court. And of 5s. from the fine of Richard Deigher for the reversion of that messuage with curtelage and three acres of land which Ibeta Menbury now holds to Hold to the same Richard as appear in the same Court. And of 36s. 8d. from the fine of John Mount senior of that land and pasture in the lord's wood of Esse which John Paull senior now holds to Hold to the same John Mount as appears in the same Court. And of 6d. from the fine of Baldwin Beram that he may dwell outside the lordship as appears in the same Court.

Total 116s.

Sum total received with arrears £24 18s. 10½d

**Deficits
in Rents.** The same accounts for the deficit in the rent of the mill of 9s. per annum. For a deficit in the rent

of Thomas Person formerly of Nicholas Fursy for
demesne land 10s. 5d. per annum. For a deficit in
the rent of · the demesne lands in le Sterte which
were accustomed to pay 27s. per annum, and now
rom so much to a less rent per annum, 7s.

Total 26s. 5d.

Expenses of the Steward and cost of . . . The same accounts for the expenses of the
steward the cellarer and others coming to the Law
Court for the term of Hock 5s 6d. For the expenses
of the Steward at the Court for the term of the Nativity
of St. John Baptist 4d. For the expenses of the
steward the cellarer at the Law Court for the term
of Michael in the following year the 18th of King
Henry who now is 3s. 3½d. Item for victuals ale
and candles from John Torre for the lord Prior
being at Esse as appeared by a tally made between
them 6s. 8d. Item delivered for the fabric of the
church of Esse for the bell tower there by the gift
of the lord Prior 6s. 8d. Item paid to· Thomas
Deygher for carrying the tithes of corn of Esse to
the barn in autumn for the task vi^{s.} Item paid to
John atte Water for railing and daubing round the
new task barn 11s. Item paid to the same John
atte Water superintending for 10 days the assistant *
stone cutters and other workmen † about the said
new barn taking per day with food 2d, 20d. Item
for one quarter of lime bought for the said barn 9d.
Item for crests ‡ bought for the new barn of Esse
21d. For one "vlage" bought for the like 3d.
Item paid to John atte Water for cutting fuel and
for other orders and husbandries done by him this
year as is declared by a bill 2s. 5½d. Item paid to
Richard Deigher for the task for making an area in
the new barn 12d. Item paid to Richard Degher for
cutting fuel in turn for the task as is declared by a bill
2s. 8d. Item paid to Thomas Deigher carrying hay
the tithes of the parish to the task court 12d. Item

---

* Adjuvantibus.
† Property tenants who do bodily service for their lord.
‡ Architectural ornaments.

to the same Thomas carrying fuel from Aysshwode to the Court 4d. Item paid to John Paul jun. for rough-casting pargend (parget, Prov. Eng.) the new barn with rubbage there 3d. Item the aforesaid John atte Watere seeks allowance by a bill for divers orders and tiling a house and cutting fuel as appears by the said bill shown and allowed 8s. 3d.

Total 50s. 9d.

Payment of Fees. Item the accountant paid to the lord of Comb fflury for a certain fixed rent per annum 7s. Item he paid to the church of Lydeard Episcopi for St. Peter's pence 4d. Item he paid to the Court of the hundred of Lydeard Episcopi for suit there released 2s. per annum.

Total 9s. 4d.

Payments of Money. Item the accountant delivered to the lord the Prior from rents and other profits this year by one tally £9 8s. 4d.

Item he delivered to dominus John Gay chaplain of Esse this year for his pension 100s.

And he delivered to the lord Prior for the fine of William Freman by the hands of the accountant 8s. 4d.

And to the same lord Prior at the audit of the account by the hands of the accountant 12s.

And to the same lord from the fine of John Munte senior by his hands 36s. 8d.

And to the same lord from the fine of Robert atte Wille by his hands 6s. 8d.

Total £17 12s.

Total ot all expenses (mis?) delivered and paid £21 18s. 6d. And so are owed to the lord 60s. 3½d. of which is allowed to the same 2s. 7d. paid to the lord at the audit of the account. And there is allowed to the same 6d. paid to Richard Deigher for fuel cut down in the lord's wood at the audit of the account. And there is allowed to the same 3s. 1½d. for the good service of the same accountant done this year and the past year. And there is allowed to the same 3s. 4d. from the amercement of Walter

Mounte pardoned by the lord at the audit of the account. And there is allowed to the same account 10s. paid to the lord the prior after the present account at the feast of the Conception of the Blessed Mary the Virgin.

Total of allowances 19s. 6½d.

And so there are now owed to the lord 40s. 10d.

Whereof upon Robert atte Wille for his fine in arrears 33s. 4d.

Baldwin Beram for his old arrears 7s. 6d.

An explanation of some of the terms used in the "Compotus," or debtor and credit account :—

Reeve.—The steward, bailiff, or reeve, probably one and the same person. The latter though obsolete still comes into the composition of titles in use as in sheriff, *i.e.*, shire reeve, or governor of the county.

He could do pretty much as he liked, and farmed the lord's demesne as if it were his own. He kept an eye on the ploughers and sowers and reapers and mowers, to see that they did their work thoroughly, in return for which he paid no rent for his own lands during his year of office, and had various perquisites. If they did not do their duty he was fined, and it was not easy to get them to do it. Sometimes the bailiff enriched himself at his lord's expense, and it was many centuries before the landlords of England learnt that there was no surer way of being imposed upon than by regarding the labourer as an inferior being and setting over him men whom they did not trust. But they did learn it eventually, and then the place of the reeve and the villein was taken by the farmer and the free labourer. The reeve was the overseer or foreman of the lord's villeins, who in every manor controlled the agricultural operations.

The inn.—The hostel of the Priory, a lodging-house for wayfarers.

Candles.—What is the meaning of these candles which John Torre supplied to the Lord Prior on the occasion of his visit to Ash Priors? Was it that Thos. Bennet, then Prior, was in the habit of sitting up late at night to prepare his sermon? He came to receive his rents and tithes and see to the work which was being done to the Church fabric and the tower, to which he contributed 6s. 8d. I do not think that was the use the candles were put to. The Prior would not have many sermons to prepare and what he did would not be written, they would be of the nature of extempory addresses, exhortations, and expositions of the duties of a true Catholic, and particularly that of giving alms to the poor and the keeping up of the Church. Even the parish priest of those days did not preach more often than once a quarter. The people of Ash Priors have never been burdened with too many sermons. The candles, perhaps, were for use at Candlemas, Feb. 2nd, the Feast of the Purification of the Blessed Virgin, so called from the number of candles used on that occasion. They were generally paid for by the parishioners themselves according to a fixed scale. Thus a man with one cow paid 12d. per annum. One with a sheep 2d. The candle played an important part in the services of the Church in those times, not only on the altar, but before images and carried in processions. Ash Priors Church is still lighted with candles on the few afternoons in the year when the daylight fails.

In grosso.—The bulk of it.

Siligo.—Fine wheat flour.

Assize.—Fixed rents.

Demesne Lands.—The fields attached to the Priory.

Tolcorn.—A percentage of grain taken by the miller for every bushel of Corn ground as his perquisite.

Heriot.—A fee of the best beast due to the lord on the death of a tenant.

Celarer.—An officer in a monastery who had charge of the cellar and wine, etc.

Peter's Pence.—By a law of King Ina every family possessed of any kind of property to the value of 20 pence throughout the kingdom of the West Saxons was charged one penny at Lammas (1st Aug.), which was sent over to S. Peter and the Church of Rome, called S. Peter's pence.

Ulage.—Probably meant for vlage, an abbreviation for villenagium. Villein tenure was the holding of land in return for bodily service on the lord's demesne. Villeins, who belonged principally to lords of manors, were of two sorts. Those annexed to the manor or land, and those annexed to the person of the lord, transferable by deed from one owner to another. They could not leave their lord without his permission, and if they ran away they might be claimed and recovered by action. They had small holdings of land to sustain themselves and their families, but it was at the mere will of the lord, who might dispossess them whenever he pleased. Instead of paying rent for their holdings they rendered bodily service to the lord of the manor. They were practically little better than slaves and were regarded as beasts. This was the condition of the labouring man at Ash Priors in the days when the Priory existed. But because this was their condition there is no reason to suppose that they were ill-treated by the monks. We have no records of our own to refer to as to the state of affairs in this parish at that time, no actual facts to quote, but we can arrive at a very correct idea of it from reference to those of other parishes at the same period. There were some Radicals in those days who "when beaten by the lord's steward for not ploughing his furrow straight enough, instead of howling as once he did, clenched his teeth and shook his fist and thought of the knights he had killed when he had gone on foreign service with his lord. It is but a forgotten incident in the most tragic chapter in the history of England—that of a futile attempt of the villeins to become free men by maltreating their masters." We should have expected the Canons of Taunton Priory to have worked for the emancipation of the villeins, but they could not well do that unless they first let their own go free. They probably treated them well enough and worked, maybe beside them, in the fields of Ash Priors, and perhaps the villeins were never nearer heaven than when they rested on their spades and hoes as the time for vespers came, and listened to the white-robed Canons at the Priory chanting their evening service.

Panagi.—The right to feed pigs on beech nuts and acorns distinguished from those fed on vegetable food. The pig at least in those days enjoyed more freedom than he does to-day, cooped up as he often is in a dirty sty, where he enjoys a miserable existence. He led a much more healthy and happy life so long as it lasted in the woods, and provided much more wholesome bacon for people to eat. The woods were valued then by the number of pigs they would support rather than by the trees they consisted of, which were of little use other than to produce beech nuts and acorns. No doubt pigs were the chief source of wealth of the village, as they are the only animals mentioned. Besides it did not pay to raise much cattle when only the lord could afford to eat meat, and the market was regulated not by demand and supply, but the price of food was fixed by Act of Parliament, and if you did not choose to sell your eggs at 24 for a penny you might forfeit them to the King.

The tenants paid their rent chiefly by ploughing, reaping, mowing, hedging and ditching for their lord, but a change had taken place by the time this account was rendered, for we find Thomas Deygher receiving vi^t from the bailiff for carrying the tithes of corn of Esse to the barn in autumn for the task.

Le Sterte.—Said to be the name of a place—of a field probably. Now we know that places took their names from people. There is no field known by that name now that I can find in the parish. In my endeavours to make something out of it I have come to the following conclusion:—How names get changed in the course of time we have an example in Street becoming Spratt, the former being in all probability the correct rendering of the name. It would be much less remarkable for Street to become Sterte.

Crests.—Architectural ornaments. There are some of these still remaining on the rockeries in the Priory grounds. They are supposed to have come off the house, but may have been the original crests here mentioned which were bought for the new barn.

Ad thuram.—It is not clear what is meant by the new barn ad thuram, or ad thaxam, unless it was so called from the tasks which villeins used to be charged with, and was the barn where the corn so reaped was stored. In any case it was one particular barn. Until quite recently and in the memory of those living in the parish there stood a barn at the corner of the field close to the Priory gate. That barn with a portion of the field was called the Parsonage Barn, probably the old tithe barn.

Hock.—A Court holden in a town on a law day called Hock Day Court, at Easter, in which, among other things, persons were elected to serve in public offices as constables, having been previously chosen by a committee of twelve worthy parishioners.

Fighting came so naturally to the people of these times that they seem to have had frequent recourse to the law courts. They could not sell a field without pretending to have a law suit over it, and then settling the matter in dispute in Court by the defendant recognising the plaintiff's right to the field he wanted in consideration of his paying him its value.

THE WINTER FAMILY.

CONTEMPORARY with the Blakes were the Winters, the latter family being even more numerous than the former.

The earliest date is the baptism of Elizabeth, daughter of Thomas and Agnis, on 21 May, 1702. During the 18th century this family appear to have lived at Ash Priors. The Winters owned a large portion of the parish and also lands in Bishops Lydeard, Combe Florey, Halse, Lydeard S. Lawrence, besides Taunton, and other places. They also owned many of the principal houses in the neighbourhood—the Priory, Watts House, Linchfield, Court House, which one by one have come into other hands. They built for themselves a conspicuous memorial in the keeper's lodge in Combe Wood in the shape of a lofty tower which easily passes for a church tower with those who only see it from the road. From the top of this tower the keeper could keep his eye on the wood, and certainly from it may be obtained a glorious view of the surrounding country. Before the Church was restored the floor was covered with slabs with inscriptions upon them. Many of them, no doubt, were much worn, and some quite illegible. One of these probably marked the vault in which the Winters were buried. The only memorial to that family besides the Church itself, which was restored in a great measure by the liberality of Mr. John Winter, is the little window in the chancel. The somewhat picturesque cottages in the bend of the road at Greenway with the turret staircase were built by them. After Miss

Winter's death the Priory was let to various tenants, and in 1900 it was bought by A. O. Saville-Onley, Esq.

There are no less than eleven families of Winters whose names appear in the registers between the years 1702 and 1802. The marriages which took place in the parish were between

Nathaniel Winter and Ann Lidworthy in 1706
Thomas   ,,   ., Mary Morse   ,, 1719
Joan   ,,   ,, John Burge   ,, 1762
Hugh   ,,   ,, Ann Totterdale   ,, 1779

Mr. John Winter and Joan his wife had the large family of eleven children baptized at Ash Priors between the years 1718 and 1742.

Charles	John	Galhamton	Edmond	Betty	Mary	Ann	Joan	Robert	Philip	Hanna*

The other families mentioned in the registers are those of

Thomas and Agnis Winter
Robert and Joan   ,,
Nathaniel and Agnis   ,,
Thomas and Eliza   ,,
Charles and Dorothy   ,,
John and Fanny   ,,

Only the two latter can be identified with the venerable John Winter and Joan his wife through their connection with the Priory.

The following obituary notice connects Charles and Dorothy already mentioned with the same family:—

" On Sunday last at Bishops Lydeard after a few days' illness, in the 28th year of her age, Mrs. Dorothy

---

* Buried at Ash Priors.

Winter, relict of Chas. Winter, Esq., of Court
House, in the same parish, and daughter of the
late Sir William Yea, Bart., of Pyrland House,
near Taunton."—*The Taunton Courier*, Dec. 2, 1813.

Later entries in the Ash Priors register of baptisms
relating to the same family :—

12 June, 1849, Fanny Gertrude, daughter of John and
    Fanny Winter, Ash Priors, gentleman.

29 May, 1856, Florence Mary, daughter of John and
    Fanny Winter, the Priory, Ash Priors, gentleman.

30 Dec., 1857, John Arundel, son of John and Fanny
    Winter, the Priory, Ash Priors, gentleman.

There are three large tombstones in Bishops
Lydeard Churchyard belonging to this family. The
oldest bears on it the inscription :—

Here lieth the body of John Winter, of this parish, gent.,
who departed this life the 2nd of June, 1762, in the 69th year
of his age. Near this tomb lieth the body of Charles Winter,
of this parish, Esqre., oldest son of John Winter, who departed this life 1796, in the 72nd year of his age.

This is the old tomb, and this is probably the
venerable John, father of at least eleven children, but
the grave of Joan, his wife, I have not been able to
discover. The other tombs are interesting, especially
the latest, which contains no less than ten names,
among them that of John Winter, of Watts House,
14th March, 1873, aged 51, at Alagoa Bay, South
Africa, interred in this vault, and also records the death
of his widow, Fanny Doidge, Feb. 19, 1907, and the
fact that she was interred at Ocklynge Cemetery,
Eastbourne.

From the *Morning Post* of Feb. 22, 1907 :—

"WINTER—On the 19th inst., at her residence, West-
    leigh, Eastbourne, Fanny Doidge, widow of the

late John Winter, of Watts House, Bishops
Lydeard, Somerset, aged 81."

After the death of Mrs. F. D. Winter, the remaining properties belonging to the Winters in this
neighbourhood were advertised for sale. The bill is
interesting on account of the names of the tenants,
particularly Ash and Tarr, names which may be found
in the registers from the commencement, John Torre
having held a messuage in the southern part of the
mill as far back as the year 1439.

Five farms with homesteads and woodlands containing altogether about 460 acres were sold on 29th
June, 1907 :—

Nethercot Farm, in Combe Florey.

Nethercot Cottage.

East Criddles Farm, in Tolland.

West Leigh Farm, in Lydeard S. Lawrence, tenant,
F. W. Ash.

Pyleigh Farm, in Lydeard S. Lawrence, tenant,
Thos. Tarr.

Winter's Farm, in Halse.

Three enclosures of accommodation land adjoining
Ash Priors Common, now occupied by Mr. John White.

Hooper's Close, near Dean Court, Bishops Lydeard.

Freehold chief rents arising out of the manor of
Hoccombe and Pyleigh.

This was the winding up of the affairs of the Winter
family as far as their connection with this part of the
country, and, when we add to this list of farms the
extensive and valuable properties already sold, we can
realize that this family were at one time the owners of
a very fine estate in Somersetshire.

My enquiries in connection with the family have
led me to the conclusion that the Winters were a

good old yeoman family who made their way up in life by a wise and careful management of their affairs; and it is probable that the little farm called Winter's Farm, lately under the auctioneer's hammer (the house belonging to it being a quaint old-fashioned little place), was the original home of the Winters. From this humble abode they moved to the Priory, and from thence to Watts House in Bishops Lydeard. In support of my idea that Winter's Farm, in the parish of Halse, was the original home of the family, I would point to the churchwardens' accounts of that parish quoted in Part III. of Mr. Montgomery's *Halse Village Notes*, in which William Wynter's name appears as one of the churchwardens.

Compot Wilhelmi Wyt at Thome Toker.

Wyllm Wyat, Thomas Toker, Wardens yn the yere of ower Lorde mcccccxlii.

Also in the year 1545: Compotus Johis Vorsey et Willmi Wynter, Wardens.

We have now to see how the Winters came into possession of the Priory and lands belonging thereto in Ash Priors.

On the 13th day of June, 1544, the King granted to Sir Francis Bryan and Matthew Coltehirste all the house and site of the late Priory of Taunton and all the lands situated in certain parishes in which the Priory owned property. They are said to be " granted in consideration of good and true and faithful services," and Mr. Thomas Hugo adds—" We need not stop to surmise its nature—rendered by these dutiful adherents." Whether it was that Sir Francis Bryan and Matthew Coltehirste entertained qualms about the nature of their perilous property must be left to conjecture. So early, however, as the year 1549, or about five years after their first acquisition of it, they procured a license for alienating it to one Thos. More. The license is dated at Westminster the 22nd June in that year. A grandson of this gentleman had five daughters, Bridget, Grace, Rachel, Gertrude and Margaret. Rachel married Hugh Bickham, Esq., in her right of the Priory in Taunton, with the manors and demesnes thereto belonging, which appear at that time to have included the manor and rectory of Ash Priors. The Taunton property was sold somewhere about 1772 and bought by Philip Winter, Esq., the uncle of John Winter, Esq., of Watts House, Bishops Lydeard. Through whose hands the Ash Priors property passed during that interval, it is not clear. Whether it was the Rev. L. H. Luxton who owned the property or some other member of the family I cannot say, but it appears from the parish records that the Priory belonged to the Luxtons immediately before it came into the possession of the Winters.

THE CHURCH.

THE chief object in every village is the Parish Church. It usually stands, as it does in ours, in the centre of the village, with the houses clustered round it. The Church tower is a landmark for the traveller, indicating the position of the village. Without it we should sometimes be unaware of its existence.

The Church is usually the most beautiful object in the village and contains all that is most treasured by the parishioners; treasures of great antiquity and works of modern ecclesiastical art. Each church has some things different from those of its neighbours —something which we point out to visitors as peculiar to our own, and from which we are able to determine the period in which it was built.

The history of our Church, as far as we can ascertain, is this: There was originally a little church consisting of a nave and chancel with a tower at the west end containing three bells. How long this building had existed before the given date, 1292, we cannot say, but we know that it was standing before that, though probably little of what then appeared now remains. The tower is the oldest part of the present structure, being of earlier date than the fifteenth century, although it may have been to some extent altered when the nave and north aisle were built, probably at the end of that century. That there was a church at Ash Priors previous to 1292 may

Holy Trinity, Ash Priors.

be gathered from the first mention of the Priory which is found in a charter by which Robert, Bishop of Bath, among the notabilia of his episcopate, converts Hywis, part of his manor at Banewell, into a prebend in the Cathedral Church at Wells. The document bears date the 29th November, 1159, and the witnesses, which constitute a very valuable list, as more than one among them are the earliest superiors of their monasteries whose names have as yet been recovered, include Stephen, Prior of Taunton. This is the earliest Prior in the list of those dignitaries, and the present is the earliest date at which he appears. The same Stephen, together with his fraternity, made to Reginald, Bishop of Bath, who governed that see from 1174 to 1191, various concessions of episcopal dues in respect of their churches and chapels; among them concessions were made in respect of Aisse. This puts the date of the Church still further back. That it is even earlier than this we know, although we can only fix an approximate date, from the gift of Robert Arundell of two hides of land and the Church and its appurtenances at Aissa, mentioned in the charter of Henry II, already referred to.

About the end of the fourteenth century the accommodation was found to be insufficient for the population and the north aisle was added. If the hagioscope existed before this was done, it must have communicated with a window in the north wall, through which people from the outside of the Church could obtain an uninterrupted view of the altar. In 1833 it was found necessary to enlarge the Church still further by the addition of the south aisle, and in 1874 the Church was almost entirely rebuilt, the chancel lengthened, and the vestry added.

The architecture of the tower represents the style of the old church. As each aisle was added the walls of the old nave were pulled down and the present arcades took their place, the windows of the north aisle being constructed in the Perpendicular style of the period, and when the south aisle was added it was made an exact copy of the north. The mouldings of the plinths of the pillars in the nave correspond with those of the pillars of the double arches in the chancel, with the difference that each side has its own style throughout. The tower, with staircase turret and battlements, similar in style to those of Berrow Church, near Burnham, without pinnacles, has single buttresses at the corners. It is said to be rather heavy for the size of the Church, but it is on that account the better able to sustain the weight of the six bells which hang therein. It has four gurgoyles at the corners, one of which is somewhat unusual, having the form of a fish, another is a demon, another an eagle and the fourth probably a lion. It is built of the local red sandstone, and has a pointed roof surmounted by a bird. Evidence that the tower is of earlier date than the Church may be seen in the arch between the tower and the nave, which is of an earlier character than any of the other arches in the Church, and further evidence may be found in the tracery of the little windows of the belfry, which belong to the Decorated period, in which the tracery, consisting of simple forms such as circles and trefoils, is known as geometrical. The tracery of these little windows will be seen to be of the trefoil form. Mr. Spencer puts the date of the tower down to the latter part of the thirteenth century, the western doorway and window, which existed before the restoration, being later insertions. He says, " I quite agree that the tower belongs to the Decorated period, but as the Church was in great part rebuilt in the Perpendicular period I came to the conclusion, after weighing all the evidence, that a larger window with a doorway under it were inserted in the tower by the Perpendicular builders, and that the tower originally had probably a small two-light window and no door under it as was common in small early churches.

"The filling in below the old Perpendicular window arch, as shown in the photograph, was quite modern, although it looks like Early English or Early Decorated work in the photograph, but such was not the case; it was of that poor character often called in derision "Carpenter's Gothic," executed by local workmen before the Gothic revival, and the sill of the window and doorway under it had evidently been tampered with in modern times."

The great west window is a reproduction of the Decorated style, in which the tracery of the upper portion of the window is pierced by the bars of stone of the same thickness as the mullions. This development was reached rather before the middle of the thirteenth century, which is in accordance with the date given of the Church in old books. Towards the close of the fourteenth century there begin to appear in the window tracery straight vertical members, and all curved lines are excluded, and the mullions themselves are continued up to the arch. These vertical lines entirely alter the character of the tracery, so that the term Perpendicular is applied to the style which may be seen in all the other windows. A marked feature of the interior is the pattern formed on the face of the walls which form the angles of the arches and the windows made by irregular stone work called quoins, which come out very clearly in the photograph. The columns of this period are described as usually treated as a group of half shafts alternating with wide shallow hollows. The half shafts only have capitals and bases, the hollows continuing up into corresponding hollows in the arch, and at the bottom dying away in the plinth. The arch being commonly blunt, the column occupies a large proportion of the total height of the arcade. The capitals are small proportionately to the small shafts which they surmount. They are seldom carved with foliage. The bases are of slight projection, but are often mounted on a high plinth. If a comparison is made with the columns which support the Gothic arches which separate the aisles from the nave, they will be found to correspond exactly with this description.

The chancel is inclined at an angle to the nave, the popular theory being that it was intended to symbolise the drooping of our Lord's head as He hung upon the cross, but the same may be noticed of the tower, and is probably due to the fact that old builders were not as careful to build as square as we do in these days. It was purely accidental.

Mr. Spencer has kindly furnished me with the following copy of a description of the work done at the restoration completed in 1874 :—

" The Church is dedicated to the Holy Trinity and built entirely in the Perpendicular style. It originally consisted of nave, chancel, north aisle and tower. A south aisle was added about forty years ago.

" During the recent restoration the chancel, which was very shallow, has been lengthened and a vestry built on the south side of it. The old north doorway, for many years blocked up, has been re-opened, and a porch added. This will now form the principal entrance, as it is the nearest one to the road. The western gallery obstructing the tower arch and window, together with the high pews, have been entirely removed. The church will now accommodate about two hundred persons including children.

" The roofs are entirely new, open-timbered and moulded, and the walls in many places had to be rebuilt and strengthened by buttresses in order to support them. Many of the windows are new, also the western doorway of the tower. Hamdon Hill stone has been used for the dressing stonework and local red sandstone for the other portions.

" The staircase to the rood loft has been retained and covered with a stone roof. An interesting feature of the old building, a hagioscope, was discovered in removing the plaster of the pier to the north of the chancel arch, and has been carefully preserved.

" The seats are of pitchpine, with carved oak ends. The chancel stalls, communion table, rail and standards are of American walnut, which gives a richness to the chancel.

" The reredos, formed of fine Corsham stone, Ham stone, white lias and marble, consists of three canopied compartments with stone diaper on each side and below. In the central compartment there is a black marble cross. The Alpha and Omega are carved in stone in the side compartments.

" The pulpit is octagonal, formed of similar stones and marbles supported by a clustered column of Devonshire marble. The font, being in a good state, has been preserved without alteration.

" The chancel is paved with Minton's tiles. The single-light window on the north side of the chancel has been filled with glass painted by Messrs. Clayton and Bell, a memorial to the late Mr. John Winter, who took an active part in the work now completed.

" The mouldings of the seats have been copied from a fragment of one of the old bench ends ; while some of the carving was suggested by a panel supposed to belong to the original rood screen.

" The mouldings upon the ribs of the roof and the bosses at their intersections were copied from fragments of the old work; indeed, wherever there has been a remnant of the old work it has been carefully studied in making the new. The tower has been repaired and pointed, and the fourth bell, bearing the date 1720, being cracked, recast. There are six bells, the oldest bearing 1711 upon it. The tenor bell is 3 foot 2½ inches in diameter.

" A chiming apparatus invented by the Rev. H. T. Ellacombe, Rector of Clyst St. George, Devonshire, has been fixed in the loft, just under the bells, by means of which the six bells can easily be chimed by one person, while it does not interfere in the slightest degree with the ordinary way of ringing when occasion requires.

" The cost of the restoration has been about £1,500, which has been raised by subscriptions with the exception of two small grants from Church building societies. Sir Wroth Acland Lethbridge and other members of that family have largely contributed, and the Vicar, the Rev. V. C. Day has been very active in raising funds.

" The contractor was Mr. John Spiller, of Taunton. The stone carving was performed by Mr. Frost and the wood carving by Mr. Spiller, junr. The whole of the works have been carried out from the designs and under the personal supervision of Mr. J. Houghton Spencer, architect, Taunton."

The Rev. V. C. Day has supplied me with the following additional information respecting the restoration:—" The Church itself, as it was, dated back to the fourteenth century and was in a very dilapidated state before the restoration, which was completed in 1874. The only alteration in the interior of the Church was the lengthening of the chancel 14 feet, which has given room for the choir seats and a small vestry, which has improved the general appearance of the interior. The whole of the interior of the Church was taken down, the outside walls remaining untouched, excepting cleaning and pointing. The Church was reseated, and a good roof took the place of the old plastered one. The font is the original one divested of the whitewash with which former church-wardens were so fond of besmearing churches in bygone times. The only events worth recording during my incumbency were the remodelling of the schools under the Education Act, the restoration of the Church and the recasting of the bells a few years ago, which has given the parish a beautiful peal of very musical bells."

A tablet on the south wall inside records the restoration which took place in 1833:—

Every house is builded by some man.
But He that built all things is God,
To whom be all Honor, Praise and
Thanksgiving for ever and ever, Amen. *Heb. c. iii, v. 4.*

This aisle was built and the church repaired at the cost and charge of Sir Thomas Buckler Lethbridge, Bart., with the consent and approbation of the Rev. Thomas Prowse Lethbridge, curate, John Skinner, churchwarden, Joseph Hobbs, clerk and sexton, and sanctioned by the gratitude of the other inhabitants of the parish, A.D. 1833.

The subject of the little lancet window in the chancel to the memory of Mr. John Winter, is Saint Andrew, and has the Latin inscription :—

Et Faciam vos Esse Piscatores Hominum. Sanctus Andræas. In Memoriam Johanis Winter, obiit Martii Die XIV MDCCCLXXIII, Annos Natus, LI.

The east window in the chancel, of which the subject is the Crucifixion, is in memory of Gertrude Elizabeth, 2nd wife of Sir Wroth Acland Lethbridge, 4th Baronet, to whom also there is a brass plate with the inscription :—

In Memory of Gertrude Elizabeth, Second Wife of Sir Wroth A. Lethbridge, Bart., and daughter of the Revd. Charles T. Mayo, of Uxbridge, who died 14 April, 1890, aged 25.

The east window in the north aisle is in memory of Anne Williams, first wife of Sir W. A. Lethbridge. This window was erected by her children, 1891. The window is by Clayton and Bell, and under it is a brass plate with the inscription :—

In Memory of Anne Williams, wife of Wroth Acland Lethbridge, 4th Bart., of Sandhill Park, and daughter of Thomas Benyon, of Gledhow Hall, Leeds, who died February 11th, 1882, aged 43.

The subjects of this window are the birth, entombment, resurrection and ascension of our Lord.

The brass tablet set in oak on the north wall bears the following inscription :—

In loving memory of Thomas Yate Benyon, late Captain 4th Hussars, who departed this life June 28, 1893, aged 33 years. This tablet was erected in affectionate remembrance by his nephews.

Passing away, saith my soul, Passing away, with its
Burden of fear and hope; of labor and play.
Hearken what the Past doth witness and say,
Rust in the gold, a moth is in thine array,

A canker is in the bud, thy leaf must decay
At midnight, at cock crow, at morning one
Certain day. The Bridegroom shall come and
Shall not delay. Watch then and pray.
Then I answered yea. *Christina Rossetti.*

The inscription round the handsome oak eagle lectern is :—

In memory of Anne Williams Lethbridge, given by Wroth and Ernest Lethbridge, March, 1893.

The Bible was " presented to the Church by Aleanore Lethbridge, 1893."

The altar plate now in use in the Church consists of silver chalice and paten, having inscribed upon them, " The gift of the Rev. Nicholas Spencer* to the Altar at Ash Priors, 1829." There is also a silver-mounted glass flagon. There is an old silver communion cup; two pewter alms dishes, marked A.P., and a stamp at the back of Robert Clothyer ; a plain brass cross ; handsome candlesticks and vases.

The cross and candlesticks are the gift of the present Baronet, Sir Wroth P. C. Lethbridge. The cross is plain polished brass, perhaps all the better for being plain; it reflects the light and is distinctly visible from all parts of the Church even when the dim twilight makes other objects invisible.

The candlesticks are very good and interesting, being old Flemish. They came out of an old church in Holland and were discovered by Sir Wroth P. C. Lethbridge in a shop in Sloan Street, bought by him and presented to the Church.

The organ, built by Messrs. Thomas Jones & Sons, Marlborough Road, Upper Holloway, London, was used for the first time on December 20, 1903, taking

*Served Halse from 1790-1840.

the place of the harmonium, "the gift of Sir John
Hesketh Lethbridge, Bart., A.D., 1870." On the
screen is a brass plate inscribed:—

To the glory of God and in memory of Sir Wroth
Acland Lethbridge, 4th Baronet, of Sandhill Park. Died
November, 1902. This organ was presented to Ash Priors
Church by his eldest son, Sir Wroth Periam Christopher
Lethbridge, 5th Baronet, 1903.

There is a stone slab in the floor near the font,
inscribed:—

Sacred to the memory of Edward Bryant, of this
parish, who died July 15th, 1802, aged 86. Also Mary
Bryant, his wife, who died May 12th, 1792, aged 72. Also
Thomas Bryant, their son who died June 12th, 1807, aged 56.

Another in the south aisle with the inscription:—

Hic Jacet Johnannis Skinner, medicus qui obijit, 12mo,
July, 1712, Ætatis Suæ, 54.

Another in the north aisle, much worn, so that
it was difficult to decipher the centre portion of the
inscription:—

Depositum

Roberti Blake, gen., et Mariæ uxoris ejus. Primus
obijit vicessimo nono Die Novembris anno Ætatis 62. Altera
Vicessimo Quinto Die Octobris Ætatis Suæ 51. Annoque
Domini Millimo Septingentessimo Quarto.

Roberti Blake, gent, Filius natu maximus Roberti et
Mariæ Blake. Hic Homo Conditur obiit Vicessimo Die
July Anno Ætatis 22nd, Anno Domini 1699.

Josephus Minimus natu Filius Roberti et Mariæ Blake.
Hic Ætiam Conquiescit vix tres habuit annos obiit 22nd
Die Septembris, Anno Domini, 1689.

Infra sunt situ reliquia Johannis Blake Armigeri Roberti
et Mariæ filii natu secundi atque Ætiam Saræ uxoris. Hic
obiit Die Vicessimo octavo Martii 1731. Illa Vicessimo
Sexto Maii, 1738.

This is the oldest monument in the Church and
has been the subject of some enquiry, but which has

not as yet led to much information respecting the family who appear to have been the old family of the place. The tablet states that the remains of Robert Blake, gentleman, and of Mary, his wife, are deposited beneath it. The first died on the 29th day of November in the 62nd year of his age, the other on the 25th day of October, in the 51st year of her age, in the year of our Lord, 1704, having previously lost their two children, Robert Blake, gentleman, their eldest, he died on the 20th July in the year of our Lord, 1699, in the 22nd year of his age, and was buried, and Joseph their youngest son, he also succumbed in less than three years. He died on the 22nd day of September in the year of our Lord, 1689. Beneath are the remains of John Blake, Esq., the second son of Robert and Mary Blake, and also of Sarah his wife. He died on the 28th day of March, 1731. She on the 26th of May, 1738.

The Skinners, who owned Pitpear Farm for nearly a century, were probably buried in the church, and the stone which bears their names, now let into the south wall outside, marked the graves of those who were buried where the south aisle now stands. It is inscribed :—

John Skinner, of this parish, July 9, 1797, 69 years.
also
John, son of above, of Pitpear, July 26, 1824, age 60.
also
Elizabeth Skinner, wife of last named, Nov. 6, 184-, 74
also
John, son of above John and Elizabeth, Apr. 20, 1859,
age 64 years.

In trying to recall the appearance of the Church before the restoration in 1874, we must leave out the present porch, now the principal entrance to the Church.

The old doorway was there, but it was blocked up, as may be seen from the photograph. The porch in which the churchwardens met Sir Thomas Buckler Lethbridge and the owners and occupiers of lands in the parish on the 26th day of July, 1833 was on the south side. They then passed the following resolutions:—" Pursuant of a notice given in the church on the 21st instant by order of John Skinner, churchwarden, it was then unanimously resolved, ' That Sir Thomas Buckler Lethbridge, Bart., having offered at his own cost and charges, to build a new aisle joining on to the south wall of the present Church, this offer be gratefully accepted. That Charles Winter, Esq., and Mr. David Acreman of this parish should have leave to build in the same aisle, pews for their own use, and the other parts of the aisle to be appropriated as the minister and churchwardens shall hereafter direct.' "

It was further resolved:—" That two of the bells in the tower should be taken down and recast, and that Mr. Wm. Pannel, of Cullompton, Devon, be employed to re-cast the same under an estimate which he has given in. Witness our hands this 26th July, 1833.

Thomas Buckler Lethbridge.	John Tucker.
Thomas Lethbridge, *curate*.	Dnl. Acreman.
John Skinner, *churchwarden*.	Edward Bryant.
Saml. Woolcott.	Thomas Bryant."
Wm. Lockyer.	

There were altogether five entrances to the Church: The great door at the west end and the present entrance at the north side, an entrance through a porch on the south side, a private entrance at the north-east corner for the use of the Lethbridge family, and a private entrance for the clergyman where the vestry now stands, approached by a flight of steps up into the Churchyard, for the convenience of the parishioners who lived at the lower end of the village.

The custom of having large square pews, for which an annual rent of 10s. a year was paid by the wealthier members of the congregarion would not conduce to economy of space ; but a reference to the census return of 1831 shows that the population of the parish was much larger than it is at present.

The stairs leading to the rood loft should have been left open. Even though there is no longer a rood screen it would contribute much to the archæological interest of the Church to be able to see the upper and lower doorways, which, with the stairs, leave no room for doubt that once there was a heavy carved oak rood screen such as we see in some of the neighbouring churches, and which we hope may one day be replaced.

I have already expressed a hope that the doorways to the staircase leading to the old rood loft may some day be opened out and good oak doors put in. I have consulted Mr. J. Houghton Spencer about it, and he says :—" I should say that the steps would probably be found if an opening were made in the wall, and my impression is that the stonework of the lower and upper internal doorways was not removed. The projection for the staircase measures, I think, 1 foot 11 inches on the outside, and the wall is 2 feet 3 inches thick, together 4 feet 2 inches. This would give space for a narrow circular staircase almost as wide as the tower staircase, which is, I believe, 1 foot 11 inches wide, measuring between the central newel and the outer wall. It is remarkable in what a small space a circular staircase can be formed. At the present time

I am having one built 2 feet wide from newel to wall in the new tower of Rockwell Green Church."

It will be noticed that the masonry which contains the staircase is angular and of no great depth. The rood loft as a rule is approached by a staircase in a circular turret, sometimes finished off at the top with battlements. In this case the shape of the projection and the shallowness of it suggest that the staircase inside may not be circular, but a straight one in the thickness of the wall, turning at right angles at the top to give access to the loft. In these cases only a slight projection, a bare thickening of the wall, is visible externally, and the lighting is either absent or by mere slits. Here it is absent altogether.

The screen crossed the north aisle and filled the lower part of the chancel archway, supporting a gallery or loft some six or eight feet wide. On the loft, or on a beam above it, stood the crucifix, with the figures of the Virgin and Saint John on either side. Parts of certain services were sung from this loft by hired singers.

The attack on the roods began in September, 1538, when royal injunctions were issued by Henry VIII ordering the destruction of images. With the accession of Queen Mary came a speedy reversion to the old uses, and the rood lofts and roods were again restored. Then came Elizabeth, in whose reign it was ordered by the Commissioners, " That the rood lofts being untransposed should be taken down to the cross beam," but happily this order for the destruction of the lofts was not everywhere obeyed so thoroughly as the previous order for the destruction of the roods.

Ignorant churchwardens were responsible for the removal of many a screen and rood loft that had escaped

Interior of Ash Priors Church.

the Protestant bigotry of the sixteenth century and the Puritan zeal of the Commonwealth period. It was at one of these periods, we cannot say which, that the rood screen and loft which was once a feature of our Church were taken down and the doors stopped up. No small attention has been given during recent years to the restoration of these screens, opening of doors, if not repairing of the roods.

The most general revival of screens has taken place and continues to do so in the West of England and in our own immediate neighbourhood, but it requires much careful thought and sound judgment to attempt . the revival or the new erecting of a worthy chancel screen.

The re-opening services on Thursday Oct. 8, 1874, were conducted in a most befitting manner, the musical portions being kindly undertaken by members of the choir of St. Mary Magdalene, Taunton ; Mr. R. Bailey, the organist at the latter church presiding with accustomed efficiency on the harmonium, a gift, by the way, of Sir John Hesketh Lethbridge, Bart., in 1874. The clergy and choir, in surplices, met at the Vicarage at 11.30 a.m. and walked to the Church singing the processional hymn 386 (A. & M.), "Rejoice, ye pure in heart." Besides the Lord Bishop of Bath and Wells there were the following clergy:— Rev. V. C. Day, Vicar of Ash Priors ; Prebendary Sandford, Combe Florey : Rev. C. J. Scratchley, Lydeard St. Lawrence ; Rev. G. R. Gilling Lax, Fitzhead ; Rev. M. A. Mathews, Bishops Lydeard ; and Rev. T. H. Sotheby, Langford Budville ; the Rev. J. Bailey (curate), Taunton St. James, and Rev. Johnson, Tolland, were also present, but not robed. Service was commenced by the Vicar, Prebendary Sandford taking the first lesson and Rev. M. A. Mathew the second ; the Rev. W. H. Walrond then continued prayers. The music employed was— for the Venite, Dr. Purcell's chant ; Psalm 42nd, No. 113 ; Psalm 48th, No. 125 ; Psalm 84th, No. 214 ; Te Deum, No. 1 ; Benedictus, No. 257 (Monk's collection). The anthem after the third collect was by Goss, "O taste and see how gracious the

Lord is " (Psalm 34). The hymn before the sermon was No. 306 (A. & M.). The Bishop preached an appropriate and impressive sermon from the 42nd verse of the 2nd chapter of Acts, " They continued steadfastly in the apostles' doctrine and fellowship, and in breaking of bread and in prayers." The sermon concluded, the offertory was collected while hymn No. 370 was being sung. Choir and clergy then reformed, and while singing recessional " O happy band of pilgrims " (No. 297) proceeded by the western door to the newly added burial ground adjoining the Church, where Psalms 49 and 115 were said antiphonally, and hymn 332, "A few short years shall roll," was sung by the choir. The Bishop, after a brief service then declared the land duly consecrated to the use of the Church of Ash Priors, as a burial ground from that day forward. The congregation, which was so numerous as to crowd the Church, then dispersed, a few strangers remaining to inspect the restored building.

Soon after the conclusion of morning service, a public luncheon was served in a marquee erected in a meadow near the Church. The Bishop presided, and was supported by the Rev. V. C. Day and the other clergy already named, Mrs. Day, Capt. Day, of West Monkton (brother to the Vicar), Mrs. Day, F. W. Newton, Esq., of Barton Grange, Mrs. Newton, Mr. and Miss Gardener, Mrs. E. A. Sanford, Mrs. Hancock, Mrs. Oatway, Mrs. Woodwark, Miss Gilling-Lax and many others.

The Bishop, in the course of his speech, said he really could not think it was mere matter of form the way in which Mr. Newton had proposed his health, and in which they had been good enough to receive it. It was one of the privileges of his position to take some small part in all the good which was being done in this day of activity in the Church. It was a great pleasure to him to see the restoration of this Church so thoroughly carried out, so that there was a place in the parish where the doctrines and rites of the Church of England would be faithfully taught and practised. Turning to the subject of restoration, he said he had lately been reading two striking testimonies (one was by Mr. Gladstone) to the fact that in no other country in the world are there any more beautiful churches than in England;

and he thought architects were now beginning to feel what had been so forcibly urged by the eminent historian, Mr. Freeman, that they should not put in a church what never existed there before, but should endeavour to restore what had crumbled away in the lapse of ages. This he thought had been aimed at with much success in the present instance.

At four o'clock a large congregation assembled in the Church, when a sermon was preached by the Rev. F. B. Portman, rector of Staple Fitzpaine. The service was choral, as in the morning, the selected hymns, &c., being as follows :— Processional hymn, 386 ; Psalms 122nd, 147th and 150th to the chants No. 322, 374, and grand chant ; Magnificat 409 ; Nunc Dimittis, 28 ; anthem after the third collect, "O how goodly," by Sir F. Ouseley ; hymn before the sermon, 164 ; after the sermon, 342 ; and recessional, 297.

The proceedings were most successful throughout and the day will long be remembered in the village. It was also a subject for general congratulation that Thursday proved to be one of the most pleasant of October days.*

---

* This account was kindly furnished by the Editor of the *Somerset County Herald*.

THE BELLS.

SATURDAY, July 15, 1899, was a red letter day
at Ash Priors. At three o'clock in the afternoon Prebendary Askwith came to rededicate the
bells. The ceremony was beautiful and impressive,
and a large congregation assembled to take part in it.
The choir were surpliced for the occasion and supplemented by members of the Combe Florey Choir. The
service opened with the Old Hundreth Psalm. The
Rural Dean standing within the altar rails addressed
the congregation: "Good people, we are met together
at this time to rededicate to the glory of God and
the use of this Church the bells which have now
been recast and rehung, for which solemn purpose let
us repair to the belfry."

The churchwardens then taking the ropes re-
quested the Rural Dean to rededicate the bells.
The Rural Dean receiving them said, "By virtue
of my office I desire to solemnly rededicate these
bells to the glory of God and to the use of this
Church separate from all profane and unhallowed uses."
Then the Rural Dean delivered the ropes to the
Vicar saying, "Receive again these bells as a sacred
trust committed unto thee as the appointed Minister
of Christ in this Church and parish, and take heed
that they be ever and only used in His service and
to His Glory."

Then the Rural Dean addressed the churchwardens
and others standing by, saying, "You are to take
notice that these bells of the Church are committed

to the custody of the Vicar of the parish, to be used only with his consent, subject to the ultimate control of the Bishop of the diocese." The bells were then raised in a peal. The service then continued with several beautiful and appropriate prayers.

I. For the ringers, that they might use the bells with reverence and godly fear, and keep themselves pure both in word and deed.

II. For the people, that when they hear the bells they may " Enter into His gates with thanksgiving and into His courts with praise."

III. For those who should be married, that they might be reminded by the bells that their vows were heard in heaven and might be led by His grace to seek the abiding presence and blessing of Him who gave Himself for His bride, the Church.

IV. For the sick, who when let or hindered from coming into the house of the Lord, may in heart and mind thither ascend and have their share in the communion of saints.

V. For the dying, that they for whose passing away from this world the bell shall sound, may be received into the Paradise of God's elect, and find grace and light and everlasting life.

VI. For those who undertook the work, that God who had put it into their hearts to do so, would bless their families and substance and accept the work of their hands. Remember them concerning this.

HYMN.   *Sychar.*

Hark on high the joyful music !
Hark the concert of the bells !
Loud their voice rings out to heaven,
Loud the praise of God foretells,

BENEDICTION.

The bells bear the following inscriptions :—

Treble.—Vaughan, Campbell Day, Vicar, 1899.

> Nos resonare jubent Pietas mors atque voluptas.

2nd.—Alianore Lethbridge, 1899.

> Whene'er the sweet church bell
> Peals over hill and dell,
> May Jesus Christ be praised.

3rd.—Mary Proctor Baker, 1899.

> Our voices sound for joy and sorrow,
> God knows which call may come to-morrow.

4th.—Original bell cast in 1730. Recast in 1874, and again in 1899 by Taylor and Co.

5th.—This peal of bells was recast and rehung in 1899 at the cost of Wroth Periam Christopher Lethbridge, W. Proctor Baker and others.

Tenor.—The old bell bore this legend :—

> Unto the church I ring and call,
> And to the grave do summon all.
>
> Recast 1899.

Each bell bears the name of the founders, John Taylor and Co., of Loughborough.

The new bell cage was supplied by J. Sully, Zinch, Stogumber.

Mr. Sully has kindly supplied me with information regarding their diameter, weight and note.

	Diameter	Weight			Note.
Treble	2 ft. 1½ in.	3 cwt.	3 qr.	11 lb.	E
2	2 ,, 3½ ,,	4 ,,	1 ,,	0 ,,	D
3	2 ,, 5½ ,,	4 ,,	3 ,,	2 ,,	C
4	2 ,, 7 ,,	5 ,,	3 ,,	5 ,,	B
5	2 ,, 10 ,,	7 ,,	0 ,,	21 ,,	A
Tenor	3 ,, 2 ,,	9 ,,	1 ,,	17 ,,	G

Inscriptions on the old bells :—

Treble.—Mr. Edward Bryant, Church Warden. Cast by C. Davis, Br—water, 1798 (28½ in diameter).

2nd.—Recast at the expense of Sir T. B. Lethbridge, 1833
    (28¼ in. diam.)

3rd.—Given by Rev. T. P. Lethbridge and other subscribers,
    1833. W. and C. Pannell, John Skinner, Church
    Warden. " Sing with melody."

4th.—Mr. Thomas Bryant, Mr. Thomas Horsey, Wardens·
    Tho. Wroth fecit 1730 (32¼ in. diam. cracked.)

5th.—John Dorborrow, Robert Nation, Wardens.
                    * FATHEVL CVPE, Rector, T.W.
    1711 (35 in. diam.)

Tenor.—   Unto the church I ring and call,
         And to the grave do summon all.
         John Skinner, W. & C. Pannell,
    Church Bell Foundry, Cullompton, 1833. (April 20,
    1871.)

We very often find three bells in a church tower.
The number three is eminently a Christian number,
and possibly that is the reason. The church towers
in Somersetshire are, however, famous for their peals
of bells, as well as for their own beauty of structure,
and we are as fortunate as our neighbours in this
respect. Particularly fortunate in having parishioners
who have been so generous in giving so liberally towards the recasting and rehanging of our bells. It is
not always desirable to recast the bells. They may,
if out of tune, be tuned by filing. But if a bell is so
far out of tune or cracked that more filing is necessary
than is consistent with the maintenance of the har-
mony and balance of the whole, it has to come down
and be recast. In this instance it was found desirable
to recast the whole peal. The inscriptions on the old
bells have been preserved, and I have given a copy of
them from the Rev. H. T. Ellacombe's *Church Bells
of Somerset*. He says, " There was a noted bell

---

*Rector of Halse, 1686.

foundry at Aish Priors carried on by Roger Semson."
It is believed to have been at a spot between the
Priory and the road which runs across the common.
" Roger Semson dedicated most of his bells to the
Blessed Virgin, and where not otherwise dedicated, he
indicates the fact by his Fleur-de-lis stop and the
legend

        † Ave † Maria † Gracia † Plena.   R.S."

That these two last letters are the initials of the
said Roger Semson is proved from a bell bearing the
same legend and the same character or type which
was found at Luppitt, in Devon, with his name at
full length set up backwards in a very different type.
That he lived at Aish Priors is proved by entries in
the Churchwardens' accounts of Woodbury, Devon,
in 1548-9, in which appear the journey expenses of
the Churchwarden on horseback, with seven men and
nine oxen going to and from Woodbury to Aish Priors
with bells to be recast, and the payment to Roger Semson, bellanter. (See *Devon Bells*, p. 282.")   T. Wroth,
his successor, lived at Wellington, Somerset, and
evidently the family intermarried with the Lethbridges.

One of the Culmstock bells also bears the same
legend, and the Luppitt bell is at once more or less
explicit on this point, on which the inscription runs,
NOSMES REGOR EM IB, which read backwards
is " Bi me, Roger Semson."

This famous bell founder is known to have made
the second bell at Monksilver, which is said to be a
pre-Reformation bell, made by Roger Semson, of Ash
Priors, in 1548-9.

The fifth bell in the tower of Combe S. Nicholas
Church has on it the same legend and the initials

R.S., which show that it was probably cast by Roger Semson at Ash Priors.

Some of the letters on the bells cast by Roger Semson are crowned, an instance of which is found in the letter N on one of the Bradford bells.

Neither of the old bells appear to have been cast by Roger Semson, but possibly the two recast in 1833 may have been his workmanship.

What authority there is for the tradition respecting the site of Semson's foundry I do not know.

In a field between the Common and Hopkins' Farm there is a deep depression of perfect symmetry overgrown with grass, which looks like a dry dew-pond, a very unusual description of pond in this part of the country. Had this hole been on the Common or even in the parish, we should probably have pointed to it as the traditional site of the foundry. But the Common has gradually been enclosed and the parishes have undergone frequent revision, and it is not at all unlikely that this field may at one time have been in the parish of Ash Priors, or at any rate that the field may have belonged to Roger Semson.

There is a similar depression in one of the glebe fields at Wellington which is the traditional site of the foundry of Wroth, the bell founder of that place, and is called by the Wellington children the roly-poly, being used by them for that purpose.

THE CHURCHYARD.

THE village Churchyard is often a sorry spectacle, cold and damp and unkempt. It is easily accounted for; the Churchyard is the parson's freehold, held in trust for the parishioners. Hence the people naturally hesitate to interfere in the matter; moreover they consider it the parson's duty to keep it in order, but to keep the Churchyard as he would like to see it is in many cases quite beyond his means. So the Churchyard would remain neglected. The parishioners would rather see the grass grow long and rank than have it grazed by sheep, which seems to be the only alternative. But mounds and tombstones make it very difficult to make a churchyard look like a garden lawn. The turf must be smooth to allow a mowing machine to run over it, and this can only be done where there are as yet no graves, or where, owing to the neglect of relatives the graves have sunk or been levelled, which has been the case very much in Ash Priors, and to which the beauty of the turf is mainly due, together with the care and labour spent upon it for many years.

The Churchyard must have been originally very small, consisting principally of the part round the Church, the larger portion being added at the time of the second restoration of the Church in 1874, when Sir Wroth Acland Lethbridge reserved the end portion for a family burial ground in consideration of his gift to the parish. How crowded this little old portion of the Churchyard must have been may be gathered from the size of it and the fact that so many persons seem to have been brought for burial from neighbouring villages and long distances. During the epidemic of typhoid fever alone, in 1841, no less than eight persons were buried in one year. It is a pleasant little burial ground, containing none of those great altar tombs so common in most old churchyards. The new portion was once a garden for growing vegetables. It is now a flower garden, and we are reminded of how that "in the place where Jesus was crucified there was a garden, and in the garden a new sepulchre wherein was never man yet laid." (S. John xix., 41.)

The members of the Taunton Cycling Club when they visited the Church on Sunday, 28th August, 1904, paid the following tribute to it :—" Having a few minutes to spare before the service we were enabled to have a look at the village churchyard, which it is pleasing to note appears to be cut as often as the Vicar's lawn, and flowers abound equally; all honour to the village authorities."

The parishioners have the good taste to prefer real flowers to artificial, and many of the graves are bright with those in season, whilst others are decorated with fresh cut flowers every Sunday. On Palm Sunday the old custom of sticking pieces of the willow (*salix capræa*), called Palms, on the graves is still kept up. The old yew tree has already been mentioned. It has been said that it was solely for this purpose of decorating and carrying it in processions on Palm Sunday that it was planted in our churchyards. It is, however, supposed that the trees often existed before the erection of churches as appurtenances to the heathen places of worship, on the site of which it is well known the early Christian churches were built. The old tree is evidently of great age and would have been a larger tree had it not been cut to give room for the weeping ash, which was planted by the grave of Mary Bradley, wife of a former vicar. This tree was probably planted in the year 1839, which is the date on the gravestone, and which makes it sixty-eight years old. This tree, with a cypress and the old yew, make a picturesque group at the north-east end of the Churchyard.

I cannot help thinking that the Churchyard at one time presented the usual features of an old English graveyard, with old grey headstones leaning this way and that, but that it never contained any of the usual altar-tombs is, I think, certain from their absence. This may be accounted for in this way. The lords of the manor lived in Bishops Lydeard and were buried there. The Blakes, the Skinners and the Bryants were buried in vaults beneath the Church and there are stones in the floor which mark the spots. There was also another vault, of which no stone marks the spot, but which is said to have been somewhere about where the lectern now stands, and that vault belonged to the Winters. When the Church was restored in 1874 it was opened, and the coffins, being exposed to the air, collapsed. It was then filled up and nothing was placed to mark the spot. Many of the headstones were moved when the Churchyard was levelled and were not replaced. Quite recently in digging a grave, a piece of a stone was unearthed with part of the inscription upon it. That stone, if I mistake not, belonged to the grave of John Middleton, gent.

THE REGISTERS.

FEW parish registers date further back than the early part of the sixteenth century, but the first order on the subject was issued in 1538, which ordered that the curate of every parish should "keep one book or register, which book he shall every Sunday take forth and in the presence of the churchwardens or one of them write a record of all the weddings, christenings and burials made the whole week before." These books seem to have been of paper, and in the course of time it was found that they were beginning to wear out; consequently in 1597 it was enacted that every parish should provide itself with a parchment book into which the contents of the old paper book were copied. The copies are generally carefully made, and the entries are usually attested by the curate of the year in which the transcript was made. It is true our old book is of parchment, and the entries appear to have been copied by a clerk and attested by the curate in this manner, but this could not be the original book referred to, for it does not commence until 1700. If registers were kept in this parish previous to this date they must either have been mixed up with those of Bishops Lydeard or lost. In 1660, at the Restoration, when many of the clergy were reinstated, many registers were never recovered from

the Parliamentary registrars to whom they had been
handed over in 1653 to be kept in safe custody·
The most remarkable thing about the old registers
belonging to this parish is that the parish or the
parson should have defied the High Court of Parliament at that time assembled and in contempt of
the King and his crown and his dignity refused or
neglected to buy a book of printed forms for marriages in 1754, but went on recording them in the
paper book. Perhaps George Farewell, who was
curate at that time, was a relation of the Bishops
Hull Farewell, and in a position to have his own
way.

Some of the men who are married between 1754
and 1757 are described as "Renter," which means
that they rented part of the Common lands, probably
for grazing. Thomas Fouracres, who married Mary
Middleton, is described as "Renter." Faithful Davridge
in 1757 is described as "Flax-dresser," which is an
uncommon occupation in this part of the country
now, but flax was grown in Ash Priors within the
memory of those living. This description is also
applied to Robert Palmer, a sojourner, in 1775, and
I find in an account of Fitzhead that flax was grown
in that parish in 1797. The old barn at Bishops
Lydeard where the lane turns up to the mill was
used for storing and dressing flax, the stalk of which
could be dressed so as to be spun into thread as fine
as silk, and used in the manufacture of linen, which
derives its name from the plant (*linum usitatissimum*)
with its pretty blue flower. The school children will
remember how in the description of the skipper's
little daughter in the poem "The Wreck of the

Hesperus," which they learnt for repetition, the words occur—

"Blue were her eyes as the fairy flax."

Linseed oil is also obtained from the seed, and, as we know, the meal of the seeds after the extraction of the oil is so valuable in sickness for poultices. The process of flax dressing was thus described to me. The heads were spread under a long table upon which the stalks were placed. The heads were then burnt so as to smoulder, by which heat the stalks were dried. When sufficiently dry they were beaten with a heavy wooden instrument, by which process the pith was extracted and the fibres separated. This fine fibre was then tied up into bundles and sent away to be woven into coarse blankets or horse cloths. At this work the children were able to assist their parents. In the weaving districts round Taunton, in the fourteenth century, every child could earn enough to keep itself by the time it was five years of age. The employed carried on the work in their own homes, for there were no large factories then as now. The weavers were scattered over the whole country and the middle man went his rounds collecting the yarn or the cloth and making his account with the capitalist in the towns.

For the safe keeping of the books it was further ordered that they should be kept in "a sure coffer" with three locks and keys, of which the parson kept one key and the churchwardens the others. The old parish chest in our Church, which is one of the most interesting relics in the parish, worm eaten, with the centre hasp broken off, but happily preserved in the chest, has carved upon it the letters, W.C.-H.H., and the date 1677.

On reference to the list of churchwardens of that date it will be seen that these letters are not far out, if we regard K and C as interchangeable letters or make allowance for bad spelling, these initials would seem to be those of the two churchwardens of that year. The chest has three locks and three keys, and each key will only fit its own lock, and thus the chest could only be opened in the presence of the minister and the two churchwardens.

THE TWO OLD BOOKS.

Described as:—i. The Register of Ash Priors, 1700; ii. The Register of Marriages of Ash Priors, 1781. From these two books Dr. Seager has made copies of all the entries of Marriages and he has kindly presented the parish with the little volume containing the extracts, which will be found in the safe. It is described as:—

Marriages at Ash Priors,

1700 to 1812,

and is prefaced with a note describing the contents and the condition of the two volumes thus:—

Volume I is a small vellum folio bound in sheep, containing Marriages, 1700 to 1781; Baptisms, 1787 to 1812; Burials, 1791 to 1812; Baptisms, 1700 to 1787; Burials, 1741 to 1790; Burials, 1700 to 1741. The entries for 1723 to 1741 are on two loose leaves of paper. In good condition, fairly clean, and in parts well written, but the entries for the first nineteen years are badly written by different clerks.

Volume II is a paper book bound in sheep, 4to size, containing written entries of Marriages (not printed forms) from 1754 to 1812, the Banns being registered on the left hand pages, 1762 to 1785. The entries in abbreviated form are continued in the first Register until 1781 when John Hammond, curate, ceased to sign the Register. There is no volume of printed forms (1754 to 1812) to be found.

The following will show how inaccurately the entries were made in those days:

Thos. Fouracres of this parish, renter, and Jane White, of the parish of Bishops Lydeard,

spinster, were married in this church by licence
this   in the year one thousand seven hundred
and fifty-four by me, Geo. Farewell, cur.

This marriage was solemnized between us

In the presence of

Although the registers commence in 1700, the first
entry in the book is an account of the yearly stipend
belonging to the Church of Ash Priors, 1780.

The Impropriator pays out of the tithes being
due the 25th January, £6-13-4. There is an
estate in the parish of Kittisford, called Little
Sutton, £8-0-0 only, containing 8 acres of land
with house and garden, orchard, etc., purchased
with the first lot of Queen Anne's Bounty, viz.,
£200. There is a second lot of the same Bounty,
viz., £200, the interest of which, £4-0-0.

John Hammond, curate.

An extract from the Estate Register of Queen
Anne's Bounty states that the governors purchased
lands situated in the parishes of Kittisford and Skilgate
for the benefice of Ash Priors.

1. Date of Acquisition, 1738. Messuage and 9½
   acres in six fields contiguous at Kittisford in
   the county of Somerset, called Suttons.

2. Date of Acquisition, 1765. Stipend deed se-
   curing £6-13-4 per annum from the Lethbridge estate.

3. Date of Acquisition, 1793. A farm called
   Yeanover, consisting of a Messuage and 31½
   acres in the parish of Skilgate in the county
   of Somerset.

When Taunton Priory surrendered to Henry VIII
the lands belonging thereto were given to various
persons, the manor of Ash Priors to John Leigh.

There still remained certain charges on these lands, payable in annuities and pensions, and a fee of £6-13-4. Can it be that this refers to the lands belonging to the Priory in Ash Priors, this being the exact sum paid by the Lethbridge estate in lieu of tithes to the incumbent of Ash Priors?

Extracts from the old registers relating to members of the Blake family between the years 1704 and 1787:

BAPTISMS.

1706 Mary, the daughter of John Blake, gent., and Sarah his wife was baptized the 17th day of January, anno predto.

1710 Robert, the son of John Blake, gent., and Sarah his wife was baptized the 24th day of May, anno predicto.

1711 Joseph Blake, ye son of Jⁿ· Blake, gent., and Sarah his wife, was baptized ye 17th day of Oct., anno predicto.

1714 Betty Blake, ye daughter of Mr. Jⁿ· Blake and Sarah his wife was baptized ye 22 day of feb., anno predicto.

1717 Anne, daughter of Mr. John Blake and Sarah his wife, was baptized ye 12th day of July, anno prd.

1720 Sarah, daughter of John Blake and Sarah his wife, was baptized the 2nd day of May, anno predicto.

1727 Susannah, daughter of Mr. John and Mrs. Sarah Blake, baptized Feb. 11th.

1747 Robert, son of Robᵗ Blake, gent., and Elizabeth his wife was baptized the 21 of January. Whom God long preserve.

1752 John, son of Robert Blake, Esqʳᵉ and Elizabeth his wife, November 12th.

BURIALS.

1704 Mary, the wife of Robert Blake, gent., was buried the 8th day of November, anno predicto.

1704 Robert Blake, gent., was buried the 6th day of December, anno predicto.

1720 Sarah, daughter of John Blake, Esq^{r..} and Sarah his wife was buried the 23rd day of May, anno predicto.

1722 Mary, daughter of Jo^{n.} Blake, gent., and Sarah his wife was buryed ye 16th of November.

1731 John Blake, Esq^{r..} buried April ye 2.

1738 Mrs. Blake, buried June ye 2.

1752 Mr. Nathaniel Blake, October ye 13th.

1762 Mr. Joseph Blake, Feb. 22nd.

1782 Robert Blake, Esq^{r..} September 12.

MARRIAGES.

1725 Luther Trott and Sarah Blake married Sept^{ber.} 3d.

1738 Mr. Richard Cridland and Mrs. Betty Blake was maried the 18th of September.

1787 The Rev. Law. Heard Luxton, of Bishops Lydeard, and Frances Blake, of this parish, widow, were married in this church by licence this 7th day of January.

Another family who have left their mark behind them by the farm still called after their name is that of the Middletons:—

On the 29th day of May Joseph Fouracre married Mary Middleton in the year of our Lord God 1702.

John Middleton and Dorothy Holey were married the 19th day of February, 1703.

John Middleton, gent., died in 1720.

Mary Fouracres died in 1759.

Joseph Fouracres died in 1779.

On the wall of Middletons Farm is a stone let into it with the initials and date, E.F., 1781. This house was for many years occupied by the clergyman of the parish, and was probably in those days called the Parsonage, or, at any rate, part of it, for it is now divided into two houses. It is a curious fact that one of the Priory fields, No. 135 on the tithe map, between this house and the Priory, is called the Parsonage Meadow. There are several other fields marked on the tithe map in the parish of Ash Priors and as belonging to the Priory, but which do so no longer, and are now in the parish of Bishops Lydeard. The farmhouse is one of those which is in the parish of Bishops Lydeard, but the Middletons appear to have identified themselves very much with the parish of Ash Priors.

LIST OF INCUMBENTS OF ASH PRIORS PREVIOUS TO THE REGISTERS.

1439. Dominus John Gay, capellanus, chaplain of Esse.
1443. Thomas Beckington, Bishop of Bath and Wells.
1463-8. Lawrence Pyle, capellanus.
1539. John Sealake, capellanus.
1593. John Still, Bishop of Bath and Wells.
1643. Edward Cook.
1662. Job Galpine, recusans seipsum legibus ecclesiasticis conformem reddere, ab hoc ecclesia amotus est.

Job Galpine was a writer of sermons which he published, and it was probably on account of the publicity thus given to his opinions that he was ejected from the benefice.

Bradbury is the name of another incumbent of Ash Priors who wrote books or about whom books were written, but I can fix no date to his incumbency.

1711. Faithful Cape, Rector of Halse in 1686, had his name upon the fifth bell.

Such a scanty list of incumbents needs some explanation, as the sequence in the large majority of Bath and Wells livings is known almost without a gap. It is quite exceptional, and would seem to mean absence of record, which of course it does; but it must be remembered that Ash Priors Church, so long as it belonged to the Priory of Taunton, was served by a "capellanus" or chaplain, and any record of these would have been kept at the Priory, of whom only three names, as far as I can discover, have been preserved. After the suppression of the Priory the parish appears to have been served by curates or incumbents of the neighbouring parishes of Halse, Bishops Lydeard, Combe Florey and Fitzhead until the year 1787, when the Rev. L. H. Luxton is instituted to the benefice.

LIST OF CLERGY CONNECTED WITH THE PARISH AS SHOWN IN THE REGISTERS.

Curates.

1754. George Farewell.
1762. John Hammond.
1779. John Farthing.
1781. David Webber.
1786. Lawrence Heard Luxton.

Incumbents.

1787. L. H. Luxton.
1811. W. Spencer.
1833. Thomas Prowse Lethbridge.
1834. Richard Beadon Bradley.

1846. Christopher Senior Lawrence.
1856. Vaughan Campbell Day.
1903. Arthur Wilfrid Baynham.

The Rev. George Farewell died at Bishops Lydeard after having served that parish for 36 years, on 11 June, 1774, as may be seen on the tablet to his memory in the niche on the wall of the south aisle of that church. The manner in which he kept his registers, omitting to obtain the signatures of the witnesses and even of the parties married enables us to form some idea of the man, and would be sufficient to account for his neglect of the order of Parliament already referred to, otherwise he appears to have given satis-faction, according to the inscription.

"Vir vere reverendus Georgius Farewell, A.M., qui in hac Ecclesia Vicarii munere per xxxvi annos fideliter functus ob. xi Junii, 1774, æt. lxvii."

The Rev. John Hammond was curate from 1762 to 1781. He was a man of strong, straightforward character, if we may judge from his bold clear hand-writing which leaves no difficulty in deciphering entries made by him; moreover he made a note of the yearly stipend belonging to the Church of Ash Priors, even if he did spell badly.

The Rev. John Farthing who made some entries in the book, incumbent of Fitzhead in 1791, was surely related to the Rev. John Farthing, LL.B., Vicar of Stogumber and Bicknoller, and Rector of Crowcombe, where he died 16 October, 1696. There is a handsome marble tablet in that church to that family.

The Rev. David Webber was rector of Combe Florey.

The Rev. Lawrence Heard Luxton came of a Devonshire family, whose home is at Brushford

Barton, near Dulverton. He became curate of Bishops
Lydeard and divided the work at Ash Priors with
the Rev. David Webber, Rector of Combe Florey.
In 1787 he became first Vicar of Ash Priors, where
he met the widow Frances Blake, and they were
married on 7th January of that year. This lady was
the daughter of Thomas Cridland, Esq., who owned
the manor of Stoke Gomer, in the parish of Stogumber.
Her brother lived at Weacombe House, near St.
Awdries. At his death the Weacombe property came
to Mrs. Luxton. The Luxtons had four children,
Eliza Frances, Catherine, Frances, and Thomas
Cridland. Catherine died when she was nine years of
age. Thomas Cridland married Miss Carew, of Crowcombe Court. Frances married Langley St. Aubyn,
Esq., of Alfoxden, in the parish of Stringston. It was
at Alfoxden House, for the place is spelt in twelve
different ways, that the poet Wordsworth and his
sister lived in 1797, and where she wrote her
romantic description of the Quantocks, at the foot of
which hill Alfoxden House is situated. "Wherever we
turn we have woods, smooth downs and valleys with
small brooks running down them through green
meadows, hardly ever intersected with hedgerows, but
scattered over with trees. The hills that cradle the
valleys are either covered with fern or billberries, or
oak woods. Walks extend for miles over the hill
tops, the great beauty of which is their wild simplicity."

Mr. Luxton was appointed incumbent of Taunton
S. James in the year 1788, one year after his appointment
to Ash Priors. He was also Prebendary of Wells, and
died in 1821. The living of Taunton S. James appears
to have been in the patronage of the Lethbridges in
those days. The Lethbridges still own the great

tithes of Taunton S. James, but the patronage of the benefice has passed into the hands of the Simeon trustees.

Altogether the history of the Luxton family from beginning to end, and their connections through marriage with members of the county families, would furnish a lot of interesting matter for a work larger than this. History points to the fact that if the Blakes were not landed gentry they married into some of the oldest county families. The Cridlands and Blakes were already connected by marriage, Richard Cridland, Esq., having married Mrs. Betty Blake in 1738.

The Rev. Thomas Prowse Lethbridge, third son of Sir Thomas Buckler Lethbridge, Bart., of Sandhill Park, was licensed to the curacy of Ash Priors on the 8th day of April, 1833; the document is still preserved among the papers in the Church chest, and by it is assigned to him the yearly stipend of £40. His name was upon the third bell which he with others presented to the Church at the time of the building of the south aisle. It is also on the tablet in the Church recording the building of the aisle. On 10 April, 1834, he married Isabella, daughter of the Rev. Thomas Sweet Escott, of Hartrow Manor. He became Rector of Combe Florey, where he died 27th June, 1851, and was succeeded by the Rev. Richard Beadon Bradley, of whose incumbency his daughter, Mrs. Barker, has given me the following short and interesting account. She says:—" We left Ash Priors in March, 1845, and I remember seeing the plans of the new house which Sir Thomas Lethbridge was going to build for my father. Of the terms of tenure I know nothing. Ash and Cothelstone were

then united, and my father served both. You will
see by the dates in the register that there was a bad
outbreak of typhus fever in 1841. It was brought
by people from another village, and my father nursed
and buried a great number. Sir Thomas bore all the
expense of medicines and extra food and drinks at
that sad time. The Church then had no vestry, there
were two large end pews at the east end, and the
communion table between them. One large pew was
the Lethbridges, and had a private door for entry.
In the summer on Sunday evenings father held little
gatherings to read and explain the Bible to the people,
and allowed them to ask questions in the schoolroom.
He began to wear the surplice when Tract 90 came out.
When we went to Teignmouth he put Mr. Lawrence
in his place. My sister, Miss Bradley, gave that carved
chancel chair when the Church was restored, and my
father taught the school children to chant and sing
instead of the old choir with bass viol, flute and
fiddle."*

The Rev. Christopher Senior Lawrence came from
Jamaica. He laid a claim to the property of Dene
Court which he was unable to establish. Though a
delicate man his three little ponies enabled him to
combine the duties of the two parishes of Cothelstone
and Ash Priors as his predecessor had done. Worry,
expense and disappointment, combined with other

---

*ASH PRIORS.—On Tuesday there died at 7, Trinity-road,
Tulse Hill, London, Mary Rose, widow of Dr. Jesse Barker, of
Philadelphia, U.S.A. The deceased lady was formerly wife of
Leander William Van Hook Starr, Aide-de-Camp, U.S. Army, and
was the eldest daughter of the late Rev. Richard Beadon Bradley,
incumbent of Ash Priors and Cothelstone, and curate of East
Teignmouth, Devon. A sister is Miss Bradley, of Crewkerne.

things, caused his health to break down prematurely, and a stone near the tower marks his grave:—

In memory of Christopher Senior Lawrence, of Tripoli, Jamaica, and incumbent of Ash Priors with Cothelstone, who died 27th April, 1855, aged 45 years.

It is a coincidence, though perhaps nothing more, that Mr. Joseph Bryant, who is buried near him, is said to have come from Jamaica, but after the Monmouth rebellion many of the rebels in Somersetshire were transported to the West Indies, from whence they never returned, but some of their descendants may have done so.

The Rev. Vaughan Campbell Day, M.A., New Inn Hall, Oxford, D., 1843, G. and B.P., 1844, B. and W., formerly Vicar of Chipstable, came to Ash Priors in 1855. Like the famous Jack Russell, in his early days he was fond of the chase, and trophies of his sporting days may still be seen on the stable door in the orchard. Mr. Day resigned the living of Ash Priors at Easter, 1902. When he was leaving the parish Eli Lockyer, the village shepherd, having a kindly thought for the shepherd of the spiritual flock, proposed that he should not be allowed to leave them without some little recognition of their appreciation of his long and faithful service in the parish.

The proposal was readily responded to by the parishioners, and accordingly a subscription was made. The present took the form of a walking stick and umbrella, which were duly presented. In a graceful acknowledgment of it Mr. Day remarked that he was much pleased with their kind thought, and added that he would find the stick useful in the fine weather and the umbrella in the wet.

THE CHURCHWARDENS' ACCOUNTS

THE history of a place is to be traced to a great extent from the tablets on the Church walls, and from the tombstones in the Churchyard, and, where the records have not been destroyed, from the parish registers and the churchwardens' accounts. In this way a word here and there may supply material for a good deal of imagination, if not facts. Unfortunately there is not much to be gathered from either of these sources in our parish. The registers do not date back far enough to be of much real interest. The churchwardens' accounts do not commence until nearly a hundred years later. They commence in the year 1793, and the book in which they have been kept from that date up to the present is bound in calf and cost 9s. 6d. From these accounts we learn that as far back as 1793 there was a clock in the Church tower. From the photograph of the old Church it does not appear to have had a face to it. In the following year a new door was required.

	£	s.	d.
For a deal to make the door under the lath		4	6
For the carriage of the deal from Taunton			6
For hanges for the door			6
For one thousand fourpenny nails ...		2	6
A presentment and book of articles ...		9	6

A regular annual charge is " Visitation fees "—

	£	s.	d.
The Minister at the Visitation ...		2	6

	£	s.	d.
My expenses		7	6

1797. For a prayer concerning taking the
Spanish ships * 1 6
For one day's work for a plough for
drawing earth and stones   ...   5 0

This entry furnishes a good illustration of how
words come to change their meaning in the course of
time. The expression is still used by the people when
talking amongst themselves, and sometimes inad-
vertently when speaking to those who do not understand the colloquial. By "plough" was originally
meant, not the instrument which turns the furrow,
but the team which draws it.

1798. The bell founder, his bill   ...   12 14 1
This was for recasting the treble bell.
For a book of prayers concerning
Admiral Duncan, taken the Dutch
Fleet † 1 6

1799. For carrying the bell to Bridgwater,
omitted in last year's account   ...   5 0
For a book of prayers concerning
Nelson's victory ‡ 1 6

1800. The clerk, his salary, and weeding
the churchyard 1 12 6

1802. For 7,000 tiles and 12 crosses, 2s. 6d.   2 2 0

This year appears to have been a very happy year,
and should have furnished the Rev. L. H. Luxton,
then incumbent, with an admirable subject for his
sermon at the harvest thanksgiving, "He maketh
peace in thy borders; and filleth thee with the flour

---

* Victory of Admiral Jervis off Cape St. Vincent.
† Admiral Duncan's victory over the French off Camperdown.
‡ Nelson's victory at the battle of the Nile.

of wheat" (Psalm cxlvii, 14).   We find the following
entries :—

		£	s.	d.
1802.	For a prayer for thanksgiving for pece		1	6
	For a prayer for a bountiful harvest		1	6
1804.	For leading the Church tower ...	12	12	0
1806.	For another new window ...	1	16	0
1807.	James Marks, his bill for pointing the tower	2	7	10
1808.	Robert Pain for new gates ...	2	1	4
1812.	Thomas Cooksley for 6,000 slat stones, 173 feet of broad slat stones, and carriage of the same... ...	4	7	0½
1813.	The glazier for repairing the windows		9	10
1814.	Mr. Newton for a bier cloth ...	5	8	0
1815-16.	Bread and wine for one communion...		6	2

1817. This year the church expenses were
very heavy. For lime, lath, nails,
lock and key, ¼ inch board 152
feet, 18 feet, 24 feet, 32 feet. Glue
and oaker, whitening, boards, nails,
deal, planks, 7 yards and ¼ and
half quarter of Dunant deal planks
and 5 doz curtain rings. Covering
stools, glazing and cleaning windows,
repairing quality binding, silk ferrit,
and making for the gallery. Then
there was William Pile, his bill,
Isaac Pearse, his bill, Mr. Cox, his
bill, James Marks, his bill, and then
Joseph Hobbs presented his bill
which amounted to £23 7s. 1½d.
alone, and a hogshead of lime omitted

the year last past; and when the churchwardens had collected £53 by 60 rates, there was still a debt of 19s. 8d. to be carried over to next year's account.

One would have thought that it would be some time before anything was required doing to the Church. The churchwarden evidently thought so too when he made the entry the following year:

		£	s.	d.
	Joseph Hobbs, another bill about the Church	1	10	0
1818.	Iron chest for the Register books	2	2	0
	Toling the bell on the Queen's burial day		1	0
	For pulling down and building up the wall against the Poor House		18	6
1819.	For two deals for the Communion railings	1	10	0
	Thomas Trott for making Communion railings	1	9	0
1820.	Mr. Thorne for the commandments and painting Communion railings and cleaning coat of arms ...	12	0	0
1821.	This year it occurred to the church clerk that no charge had been made for oiling the clock for the last seven years		4	8
1822.	A plough 2¼ days drawing rubble		17	6
1823.	George Hembrow for 6 loads of stones		6	0
	James Marks, his bill about the wall	2	1	5
1824.	3 days work on the churchyard wall		3	6
1825.	Thomas Cooksley, for 1500 tiles		7	6

		£	s.	d.
1826.	New Surplus	2	5	0
1827.	Tolling the bell for Duke York ...		2	6
1829.	Ringers for 5th November ...		5	0
1831.	A prayer for the disturbed state of the country (at the time of the Reform Bill and the riots in consequence)...		2	6
	Thos. Trott, bass viol strings ...		5	0
	Two prayers for the collera morbus		5	0
1832.	A prayer for a general fast (for collera)		2	6
1833.	Two bells were recast this year by Mr. Pannell, of Collumpton, towards which Sir T. B. Lethbridge contributed £10.	39	10	0
1834.	Hitherto three communions in the year had been the custom of the place. This year there were four, in 1841 six, thenceforth more frequent.			
1836.	The debt on the bells is paid off	5	14	7
1839.	8 loads of building stones ...		9	6
	James Marks, repairing churchyard wall	2	14	8
	Mr. Cooksley, for 2,500 tiles ...		11	10½
	Carriage of do. from Okehampton		6	3

I have selected a few items out of a great number, sufficient to show the care our forefathers took of their Church, and how they raised the money and laboured to maintain the fabric which they have handed down to us. The windows, the walls, the roof, the tower and the bells needed constant repair; every year there seems to have been work going on at the Church. How was that, was it that the workmanship of those

Ash Priors Church in 1873.

days was so much inferior to that of our own? I think it was due to the fact that they were engaged in patching up an old and dilapitated building, which was ready to fall to pieces, the greater part of which was eventually pulled down and rebuilt. These repairs were met by rates ranging from 4 to 60 in the year. The last rate was collected in the year 1868 at 2¾d. in the pound. After this the expenses were met by subscriptions. The offertory system commences in 1896.

"On Lady-Day, 1827, Miss Sarah Fouracres, of Bishops Lydeard, agreed with the churchwardens and others of Ash Priors, to pay to the said churchwardens yearly the sum of ten shillings and sixpence for a seat or pew in the Church of Ash Priors, adjoining Mr. Skinner's pew, which sum is to be laid out towards the repairs of the said church, and we the undersigned consent to let her the said pew accordingly. The first year to be payable on the 25th day of March, 1828.

JAMES TREBLE, *Churchwarden.*
JOHN SKINNER."

"May 15th, 1828, Paid Mr. Treble, churchwarden, the sum of ten shillings and sixpence, according to the above agreement.

SARAH FOURACRES."

I close the churchwardens' accounts with the reflection that they contain nothing of great interest.

Like the registers, they do not go back far enough. No mention is made of roods or pixes, or images or candles, they belong to an earlier period than that comprised in these accounts. The period to which they relate is rather that of whitewash, glue and ochre, strings for the viol and such things, when the Psalms had been set to the new version by Messrs. Tate and

Brady, and Mr. George Tarr, within the memory of the older residents, gave out from the gallery, at the west end of the Church: "Let us sing to the praise and glory of God the first Psalm," and read out verse by verse:

> How blest is he who ne'er consents,
>   By ill advice to walk;
> Nor stands in sinners' ways, nor sits
>   Where men profanely talk.

And then, drawing out the long reciting note upon the viol, young men and maidens, old men and children sang with a heart which has long since departed.

Nevertheless, I congratulate the churchwardens of those days on the neat and accurate manner in which they kept their accounts for more than a century.

List of Churchwardens.

1677. William Kerswell and Henry Hall.
1706. Thomas Winter and John Cornish.
1714. Robert Nation and John Durborow.
1716. Robert West and Thomas Horsey.
1720. John Cornish and Thomas Hill.
1733. John Skinner and Thomas Bryant.
1736. Robert Hallett and John Hall.
1738. Thomas Bryant and William Rosseter.
1742. Robert Blake, Esq., and John Hall.
1751. Edward Bryant and Joseph Fouracre.
1768. Nicholas Durborow and John Skinner.
1773. Richard Venn and John Cross.
1777. John Tucker and John Ash.
1789. Rev. L. H. Luxton and Edward Bryant.
1793. John Hurford and Joseph Hill.
1796. Edward Bryant, junr.

1799. Edward Bryant, junr., and John Hill.
1802. John Hill.
1808. John Skinner.
1810. William Bryant and Edward Bryant.
1820. Edward Bryant.
1827. John Skinner and James Treble.
1851. John Winter.
1853. Samuel Woolcott.
1880. James Parmenter.
1883. Sir Wroth Acland Lethbridge, Bart.
1897. W. Proctor Baker, Esq., and Edwin Bryant.

LIST OF OVERSEERS OF THE PARISH.

1677. William Nation and John Hiccorry.
1706. Ann Sansom and Nathaniel Winter.
1714. John Middleton and John Cornish.
1720. Robert Nation and Mary Skinner.
1733. Robert Love and Robert Hallett.
1736. Ann Sampson and Thomas Horsey.
1737. William Hobbs and Joseph Fouracres.
1742. Robert Blake and John Hall.
1751. Edward Bryant and John Hall.
1766. Nicholas Durborow and John Skinner
1777. John Tucker and John Ash.
1789. Rev. L. H. Luxton and Edward Bryant.
1792. Elizabeth Fouracre.
1793. John Hurford and Joseph Hill.
1799. Ann Hill.
1812. Edward Bryant.
1814. William Bryant and John Skinner.
1815. John Hill and Edward Bryant.
1825. William Lockyer and John Tucker.
1834. William Lockyer and Charles Dyer.

List of Church Clerks.

Nicholas Furse, died Nov. 21, 1793.
Joseph Trott, appointed   ... 1793.
John Lockyer   „   ... 1803.
Joseph Hobbs   „   ... 1827.
Thomas Hobbs   „   ... 1839.
John Tarr   „   ... 1897.
John House   „   ... 1900.

THE LETHBRIDGE FAMILY

SANDHILL Park, the seat of the Lethbridges, stands in the parish of Bishops Lydeard. It was formerly known as the Hill House. It was after it assumed the proportions of a mansion that it acquired the more dignified name. It is often said that part of the house is in the parish of Ash Priors; that it is so may be seen on the map. That portion of the park and the water shown in the illustration are in the parish of Ash Priors. The latter is called in the tithe map, "the fish pond." Part of the lake is also in the parish. Although the house is not entirely within the limits, the Lethbridges claim a large space in my sketch of Ash Priors, being lords of the manor, patrons of the living, owners of the tithes, and all along closely identified with the place and the Church in which they have worshipped for generations. I shall now proceed to give a brief account, I will not call it a history, of the Lethbridge family. This will take us back quite as far, if not further, than the history of the parish. A glance at the extract from the family pedigree will show that they were a Devonshire family, and it was not until the year 1755, as will be seen, that at the death of John Periam, Esq., they became possessed of property in Somersetshire.

The family of Lethbridge is one of great antiquity, claiming descent from Lothbroke, a noble Dane. From

Prince's *Worthies of Devon* I find the following story in connection with this man. Hawking one day on the sea-shore, his hawk took her flight seaward, and he taking a little cock boat to follow her, was driven by contrary winds to the coast of Norfolk, and there landed at Rodham, where by King Edmund he was so well entertained as to raise the jealousy of one Beric, the king's falconer, who murdered him in a wood. Beric was convicted of the murder and punished by being set in Lothbroke's boat without sail or tackling. Thus by wind and tide he was driven over into Denmark to the very place where Lothbroke had taken the boat, by which he was identified, and accused of the murder; but very falsely and maliciously he told them that King Edmund had murdered Lothbroke. His story was believed and the king of Denmark was glad of the excuse to invade England. Under the command of the two sons of Lothbrooke, Hunga and Hubba, and under the auspices of the banner which had been worked during one moontide by the hands of their three sisters, which they took with them, he sent an avenging army. This banner, consecrated after the horrid rites of Pagan superstition, was believed impossible to be taken, and the reafen, or raven worked upon it was thought to have the power of predicting the good or evil success of any enterprise by the motion of its wings. This banner was consulted previous to any serious undertaking and the assurance that "the raven had flapped its wings" gave confidence to the Danes. The Danes were eventually defeated by King Alfred at Kinworth, near Appledore. At Hubblestone, in a bend of the road between Northam and Bideford, there is a stone let into the wall which marks the traditional spot where Hubba was slain. Upon it is the inscription:

Near this spot lies buried King Hubba the Dane, who was slain by King Alfred the Great in a bloody retreat A.D. DCCCLXXXII.

Saxon Q.H.R.O.N.I.O.N.I.E.

Chappell's Record.

From this road there is a fine view of Westward Ho! and the foreshore, where it was easy to imagine the landing of the Danes and the routed army being swept back into the sea by Alfred's victorious troops.

The defeat and capture of the reafen struck such terror into the minds of the Danes, as very greatly to dispose them shortly after to make peace with Alfred, who, instead of driving them out, allowed them to settle in the country. We might have expected to find the family crest of the Lethbridges a raven, rather than an eagle with wings spread.

I have only traced the Sandhill branch of the family from the pedigree kindly lent me by Sir Wroth Lethbridge with a series of illustrations of the homes of the different branches of this old Devonshire family, among them being one of the picturesque old 16th century manor house at Pilton, near Barnstaple, called Westaway, the home of the first baronet, and acquired through marriage by Christopher Lethbridge in 1681. Of this branch, Sir Wroth Periam Christopher Lethbridge is the head. The other branches with which we are not immediately concerned are the South Tawton, Winkleigh, Jacobstowe, Exbourne and Hatherleigh branches. Their monuments may be found in these churches. A latin inscription in Farringdon Church, near Exeter, describes the family as originally Danish, whilst those to the memory of the Sandhill branch will be found in Bishops Lydeard Church and latterly at Ash Priors.

Christopher Lethbridge, born at Walston, in the parish of Clanaburgh, near Okehampton, was brought up in the City of Exeter, where he made his fortune and rose to high position. He became mayor of that city and by his last will, dated November 21, 1669, gave an annuity of £3 os. 8d., issuing out of his dwelling house situate in the parish of St. Mary Arches, to be paid quarterly during the term of 3,000 years, that the same be bestowed in a middle sort of bread, by equal portions by the churchwardens of the parish, distributed every Lord's day among 14 poor people; so that all the poor of the parish might partake of this charity they were enjoined not to give the bread to the same poor people two Sundays following, but as it came to their turns.

He also founded alms houses within the south gate of the city and parish of Holy Trinity for six poor people, allotting them the yearly sum of £15 12s. for ever, to be equally divided amongst them once a month, one of the said six to be of the parish of St. Mary Arches.

At the eastern end, in the centre of the nave, near the choir screen of the Cathedral there is a brass plate let into the floor. Upon it are the motto, "Spes mea in Deo," and the words, "Sacred to the memory of the Lethbridge Family."

I gather from the monuments in Bishops Lydeard Church that there lie in the family vault there under the north aisle:

Jessinthina Anne Lethbridge,
John Periam,
Elizabeth Periam,
Sir John Lethbridge,
Dame Dorothy Lethbridge,

Jessie Catherine Lethbridge,
Elizabeth Cannon, daughter of Christopher
    Lethbridge,
Sir Thomas Buckler Lethbridge,
Harriett Rebecca Lethbridge.

To the last is an elegant tablet with female figure leaning against an anchor with inscription giving the date of her
death at the age of 27 years and nine months, and a verse:

"Reason may soothe, but strives in vain to heal
The pang which husbands, friends and parents feel,
When thus the fair, the young, their joy, their boast,
Elude their grasp and moulder into dust ;
Faith, faith alone, those balsams can supply,
That faith which tells us we can never die,
Which tells us death his conquests shall restore,
And all the just shall meet to part no more."

Harriet Rebecca, wife of John Hesketh Lethbridge,
died at Cheriot Lodge, near Dunster, March 13, 1826.

The pedigree of the Lethbridges is traced back as
far as 1199, to Oger de Lethebroke, of Lethebroke,
co. Devon, from whom follow eleven down to—

John Lethbridge = Alienor Westlake
Thomas Lethbridge = Elizabeth, 1580.
John Lethbridge = Zenobia Stafford, of Stafford,
    1595.
Rev. John Lethbridge = Mary Reynolds.
   Vicar of Ashprington.
Christopher Lethbridge = Margaret Bouchier, 1681.
Thomas Lethbridge — Sarah Periam, 1719.
  of Westaway, co. Devon.   Daughter of John Periam, of
                Milverton, Som.
John Lethbridge = Grace Carder, 1744.
Sir John Lethbridge = Dorothea Buckler, 1776.
Sir Thomas Buckler = Jessie Catherine Hesketh, 1796.
Sir John Hesketh = Julia Hugh Hoare, 1827.
Sir Wroth Acland = Ann Williams Benyon, 1861.
Sir Wroth Periam Christopher = Alianor Chandos Pole, 1892.

From the pedigree it will be seen that Thomas, son of Christopher Lethbridge, of Westaway, married a daughter of John Periam, of Milverton, Esq. John Periam, having no son, left his property, which included the Sandhill estate, to his grandson, John Lethbridge, and thus Sandhill Park came to the Lethbridges.

The Periams were a Devonshire family, descended from Sir William Periam, Knt., Lord Chief Baron of the Exchequer in the time of Queen Elizabeth, of which no traces any longer remain in that place, except the slab in the Church over the vault. Upon this slab is carved the family arms and the inscription :—

Here lieth ye body of Zacharia Periam, who dy^d May ye 13th, 1738, aged 35 years. Also Sarah Hiles, wife of William Hiles and daughter of the above Zacharia Periam, who died —— 31st, 1827, aged 89 years.

John Peryam, sometime Mayor of the city of Exeter, by his last will, written in 1571, gave to the Mayor, Bailiffs and commonalty of the same, £100, to be lent to two young merchants thereof without interest for four years. This charity was increased by his son, John Peryam, in 1616 by a sum of £1,000 and a silver basin and ewer to be ordered and disposed of by them for ever, so that £100 should be spent to defray the city's debts and the rest upon each S. Andrew's day should be lent to five merchant adventurers trading beyond the seas, especially those of the meaner sort who had not been engaged in retail business, or bankrupts, or compounded with their creditors for less than they were able to pay.

Portraits of John Periam and Mrs. Periam, by Hudson, may be seen at Sandhill Park, and there is a tablet in Bishops Lydeard Church :—

To the memory of John Periam, Esqre., who died Jan. 16, 1755, aged 54 years, and was buried the 31st of the same month.

In these days of quick burial it is worth noticing the long interval which elapsed between the day of his death and that of his funeral. His wife, Elizabeth, also died and was buried in Bishops Lydeard Church, to whom are ascribed conspicuous virtues. She was

In piety truly Christian, in charity liberal, in friendship sincere, benevolent to all. She was the daughter of John Southey, of Fitzhead, Esqre.

Besides Thomas Lethbridge, who married Sarah Periam, Christopher Lethbridge had a son called after his own name, who married Mary Cannon, of Bishops Lydeard. Their only daughter, Elizabeth, was called after her mother. She was possessed of virtues even more numerous than those of her aunt which are recorded in a Latin inscription in Bishops Lydeard Church where she is buried.

Elizabethæ Cannon, Viri honorabilis Hugonis Somerville Honoratissimi Domini Jacobi Baronis Somerville filii natu Secundi delectissimæ Simul amantissimæ uxoris Christopheri Lethbridge de Westaway in agro Devoniæ Armigeri et Mariæ uxoris sobolis unicæ. Quæ puerperii casibus succumbeus propinquis æque ac amicis flebilis occidit fuit inim (Si alia quæpiam valide amabilis oris placidi, Sermonis, Suavissimi, Integritatis pristinæ, Sed virtutes suas non est hujus marmoris annumerare quæ ac quantæ fuerunt, dies supremus indicabit obijit die quarto octobris, An. Sal., 1765.

Sacred to the memory of Elizabeth Cannon, only child of Christopher Lethbridge, of Westaway, in the county of Devon, Esqre., and Mary his wife, at the same time the most charming and beloved wife of Hugo Somerville, second son of the Right Hon. James Baron Somerville, who died in child birth. Equally lamented by relatives and friends, was among other things, very lovable, of dignified appearance, of pleasing address, of a past integrity, but it is not the part of this marble tablet to enumerate her virtues, what and how many they were the great day will disclose. She died on the 4th of Oct., in the year of our Salvation, 1765.

There is an interesting circumstance connected with the family which is preserved by an old silver drinking cup which is in the possession of one of the members of the family, once owned by John Lethbridge in 1715. It has engraved upon it the arms of the family and a diving bell. That "necessity is the mother of invention" is an old proverb, and it finds an illustration here.

John Lethbridge appears to have been a man of moderate means; indeed he came into straitened circumstances and had to look this way and that in order to make both ends meet. Being of an inventive turn of mind he conceived the idea of a method of recovering the hidden treasures of the deep. For this purpose he procured an empty wine butt, which he made air-tight, and discovered that he was able to remain under it for a considerable time. Then he put it under water and found that he was able to remain for even a longer space of time under water than above. These experiments led to the further development of his ideas and the invention of the diving bell.

John Lethbridge, in the year 1776, married Dorothea, daughter (and co-heiress with her sister Mary, wife of Sir Francis Dugdale Astley, Bart., of Everleigh, Wilts) of William Buckler, Esq., of Boreham, in the same county. He was created Baronet on 15th June, 1804.

Sir John Lethbridge now enjoyed the Sandhill property besides the great wealth with which his ancestor, Christopher Lethbridge, had endowed the family, and which enabled him to render that valuable assistance to the King in those troublous times at the beginning of the 19th century which gained for him the family honours. He came to Sandhill in 1767, and it was

in all probability at that time that the house was enlarged and the walls hung with the pictures which
may be seen there, and which include valuable examples
of Salvator Rosa, Poussin, Guido, Vanderbilt, Snyders,
Sir Joshua Reynolds and Gainsborough, and the shelves
in the library received many of those ancient books of
which there is a large collection. There is a portrait
of the 1st Baronet. He died at Sandhill, and the
tablet in Bishops Lydeard Church states :—

Underneath are deposited the relics of Sir John
Lethbridge, Bart., who departed this life 15 Dec., 1815, in
his 70th year. He had resided at Sandhill Park in this Parish
for the last 48 years, but was formerly of Westaway House,
in the county of Devon, where, and at Winkley Court, in the
same county, his ancestors had been for many generations
situated. This stone is also sacred to the memory of Dame
Dorothy Lethbridge, relict of Sir John Lethbridge, Bart., and
elder daughter and co-heiress of the late William Buckler, of
Boreham, in the county of Wilts. She lived a pattern of
Christian piety and virtue, and died full of good works Dec. 1st,
1831, aged 82 years.

Sir John Lethbridge was succeeded by his eldest
son, Thomas Buckler, born 21 Feb., 1778, who lived
at Sandhill and took a lively interest in the parish
of Ash Priors and its Church, the south aisle standing as a monument to his memory. In 1796 he
married Jessie Catherine, sister of Sir Thomas
Dalrymple Hesketh, Baronet, of Rufford Hall, Lan-
caster, who died at the early age of twenty-five in
1801. In 1803 Sir Thomas married Anne, daughter
of Ambrose Goddard, Esq., of the Lawn, Swindon,
Wilts. Sir Thomas was a great politician, and he
represented the county of Somerset for more than
twenty years in Parliament. The bitter sarcasm of
his opponents speaks more loudly than anything for

Sir Thomas' powers of speaking. Here is an extract from one of his political speeches: "First, modestly insisting that because there was now no opposition to him it was a decided proof that his sentiments were those that were entertained by the great majority of freeholders. You wish me to say (he proceeded) more particularly what those principles are. I answer in three words—Church and King, by which I mean that it is my intention to make the basis of all my political conduct the entire preservation of our glorious establishments, whether of Church or State, the main pillar of which is, in my mind, the Protestant ascendancy in all matters, whether of a religious or political nature. And in order to effect this (as a preliminary indispensable) I certainly shall give, as far as my humble abilities will enable me, the most decided opposition to the admission of Papists to political power." The editor of the paper which recorded this speech, commenting upon it, says, "Sir Thomas continued in this enlightened strain through the whole of his speech, leaving his hearers at the end as much in ignorance as ever as to what were his principles." There are two portraits of Sir Thomas at Sandhill, one representing him in the days of his youth, an exceedingly handsome man, and a full length one on the stairs with his favourite horse, when he has grown old and grey but still retains his good looks. Another portrait of a lady named Anne Lethbridge is evidently his second wife, the daughter of Ambrose Goddard, Esq., contrasting with her mother-in-law, the slight pale-faced Dorothea Lethbridge, whose portrait hangs near. Sir Thomas took an active part in local affairs besides political, and it was to his influence and exertions with others that the West Somerset Savings Bank was established at Taunton on the 6th of September, 1817. The advantage of this institution was recognised by the class of persons for whom it was intended, and the number of those who availed themselves of it from its commencement to the 6th of September, 1821, was 2,653, and the sums deposited with the interest thereon during that period amounted to £89,897 12s. 8d. But although Sir Thomas had encouraged economy in others and taught them to put their money into the Savings Bank, he was not as careful himself, but invested his own in more speculative concerns.

It was the little mineral railway which runs from Watchet to the Brendon Hills, now overgrown with grass and weeds, in which he had shares and which looks so very unlike paying a dividend. The Brendon Hill Iron Works were opened in 1851. According to a local story a gang of Welsh miners in clean white smocks and with bright new picks and shovels were pointed out to him as the men who were ready to dig gold out of the Welsh hills for him, and proved a decoy. Sir Thomas wrote a diary, and it is a matter for much regret that his diary was not preserved; it might have furnished much useful information for the historian, as he was in the habit of recording, besides events, conversations which took place between himself and others. No doubt his executors regarded the pages of an old diary as so much rubbish, but papers of no legal value are often of great historical interest, and it is a pity they were consigned to the flames. Sir Thomas died at Bath and was buried at Bishops

Lydeard. The sexton kindly supplied me with a
ladder to enable me to copy the inscription on the
brass plate on the wall of that Church :—

To the memory of Sir Thomas Lethbridge, Baronet, of
Sandhill Park in this Parish. He departed this life on the
17th day of October, A.D. 1849, aged 71 years. His remains
lie buried in the vault beneath this Church.

John Hesketh Lethbridge, as his name indicates, was the son of Sir Thomas and Jessie
Catherine. Born in 1798, he married in 1817 Harriet
Rebecca, daughter of John Mytton, Esq., of Halston,
Salop. This was the romantic marriage referred to
later on, but it was not destined to be a long union,
for ten years later Sir John marries Julia, daughter
of Sir Henry Hugh Hoare, Bart.

Sir John lived at Sandhill. According to his
own account it was his father's wish that he should
be ordained. It is not to be wondered that the heir
to a title and broad lands should not have responded
to this wish, even if the family living had been one
of those in which the Rectory house and grounds
seem to be more fitted for the squire than the parson.
The wish to have a son in the Church was realized
in a younger son, the Rev. Thos. Prowse Lethbridge.

There is a magnificent full-length portrait of Sir John
Hesketh in the hall at Sandhill, and in the same
picture by his father, who stands by the side of his
horse, sits a little boy. This boy is Albert Arthur
Erin, born in Ireland in 1840 ; he married a Cana-
dian lady and died out in that country. The town
of Lethbridge in the province of Alberta takes its
name from the Lethbridge family.

In 1855 Sir John married his third wife Anna,
daughter of Robert Wright, M.D., First Physician of

Sandhill Park.

Greenwich Hospital, Physician to the Dukes of Kent and Sussex, Surgeon to William IV. when Duke of Clarence. Sir John was the nineteenth in direct descent from King Edward I. He should have been succeeded by Thomas Christopher Mytton, Lieutenant in the 85th Regiment, but for his untimely death from yellow fever in 1844, at Brimstone Hill Barracks, Saint Kitts, which left it open to his brother, John Periam, to succeed. He, however, did not outlive his father, and thus Wroth Acland, the eldest son by the second marriage, succeeded to the title. Sir John Hesketh was the father of eighteen children. During the latter portion of his life he lived at Ilfracombe. Whether it was the place which had a fascination for him and the old neighbourhood from which the family originally came, or the endeavour to retrieve his family's losses by a quiet life at Ilfracombe whilst Sandhill Park was let, I do not know, but with reference to the latter, a little story is told of Sir John, who had to bear the consequences of his father's misfortunes, which shows that a vein of humour mingled with even his more serious thoughts. At the level crossing over the railway, near Watts House, may still be seen traces of a track which led up to a little farm which once stood near the spot known as Marks, from the name of the occupier.

When the old man was breaking up and approaching the end of his days, Sir John one day paid him a visit, and in course of conversation said to him, " Well, Mr. Marks, you will meet my father before I shall, be good enough, if you please, to tell him that Sandhill Park is still not out of debt." In the churchyard of the parish church at Ilfracombe is the tomb where himself and his wife and daughter are buried. Near it is the iron seat upon which he sat to superintend the construction of the tomb which was all prepared before hand, leaving only the names and dates to be filled in when the time came.

On the 16th and 17th of June, 1907, I made a cycling expedition from Ash Priors to Ilfracombe in order to copy the inscription on this tomb. The distance is 59 miles. On my way I passed through Bampton, South Molton, Swimbridge, and Barnstaple. At Swimbridge I had an interview with the old postman of the village, who knew the Rev. Jack Russell well. He related to me several stories connected with that worthy gentleman. The thing which commended him most of all to his esteem was that though a clergyman of the Church of England, he was always most friendly with him, a Nonconformist. An incident illustrating Russell's devotion to duty as well as sport was on the occasion of his father's death, who by the way was, of course, a Nonconformist. Being at a distance at the time, he heard the old man was dying. He immediately mounted his horse and rode. He arrived at the house in time to see him alive; but, added the old man, the horse! Well, he would not say that it died, but if it had it would not have been the first horse that had died under the Rev. John Russell.

I stayed at Barnstaple for the night and found in the Golden Lion Hotel, where I put up, another link in the history of the Lethbridge family. The landlady told me that the old house had once been the private property of the Bouchiers, Earls of Bath. It will be recollected that Thomas Lethbridge, who married Sarah Periam, was the son of Christopher Lethbridge by his marriage with Margaret, daughter

of Philip Bouchier, Esq., of Tawstock, Devon, in 1681.
The ceiling of one of the rooms contained some
beautiful old mouldings with curious representations of
scripture subjects, viz., Adam and Eve, the Sacrifice
of Isaac, the Annunciation, and the Nativity. At
Pilton again, about a mile out of Barnstaple, on the
Ilfracombe road, was Westaway House, the home of
Christopher Lethbridge. The house lies low on the
left hand side of the road; it has quite recently been
restored by the present owner of it, C. H. Bassett, Esq.
The present occupier told me that before it was
restored it was three cottages, which have been made
into one house with a new frontage, representing an
old manor house of the sixteenth century. It is a
little disappointing to find that the date 1634 inside
the porch is not the date of the house, but it is
probably approximately correct. On the outside over
the entrance is a modern sundial, upon which is
engraved :—

This porch was erected in 1888 with materials taken
from an ancient manor house in the village of Berrynarbor,
part of which was in ruins.

Tempus Fugit.

The beautiful old church at Pilton is full of the
monuments of the Lethbridge family, notably a very
handsome one of Devonshire marble with the coat of
arms of the family and other quarterings. This tablet
is to the memory of Christopher Lethbridge, and it
is dated 1713, with a Latin inscription. The monument is endowed for its perpetual preservation, and
also the roof of the south aisle in which it is placed.

There are also monuments to

Thomas Lethbridge, son of Thomas Lethbridge, of Clements INNES, younger son

of Christopher Lethbridge and Margaret,
daughter of Philip Bouchier   -   - 1744
Christopher Lethbridge   -   .   - 1746
John his nephew   -   -   -   - 1761
Grace, wife of John -   -   -   - 1780

There are also monuments to the Whytes. Un-
happily Westaway House was sold in 1817 by Sir
Thomas B. Lethbridge to John Whyte, Esq., who
owned it for many years, from whom it passed into
the possession of its present owner. Philip Bouchier,
Esq., and Agnes his wife, the former owners of
Westaway House, are also buried there, 1687.

The tomb at Ilfracombe is of white marble covering an area of 15 feet by 12 (enclosed by iron railings).
Close by is the iron seat with a plate upon it stating :
" This chair was presented by Sir John Hesketh Lethbridge, Bart., A.D. 1872." The tomb bears the
following inscription :—

Sacred to the Memory of
Sir John Hesketh Lethbridge, Bart., J.P. of Dorset, of
Sandhill, Park, Somerset, died March 1st, 1873, aged
74 years.
And Anna his wife, died July 14th, 1880, aged 74 years.
Simply to the Cross we cling.
SUNSET—SUNRISE.
Contemplate when the sun declines
Thy death with deep reflection ;
And when again he rising shines,
Thy day of resurrection.   *Cowper.*

To the left is a polished grey granite recumbent
cross inscribed :—

Grace Catherine Lethbridge,
Daughter of Sir John Hesketh Lethbridge, of Sandhill Park,
Somerset, died July 31, 1871.

Sir Wroth Acland Lethbridge was born on 2nd Jan.,
1831. He entered the army and was Lieutenant in the

Rifle Brigade. On his marriage in 1861 with Anne Williams, daughter of Thomas Benyon, Esq., of Thorp Arch, Tadcaster, he resigned his commission and resided for five years at Upper Hare Park, near Newmarket, then at his own house, The Lodge, Six Mile Bottom, in the same neighbourhood. Upon the death of his father in 1873 he succeeded to the title and came into possession of Sandhill Park. The beautiful Lady Lethbridge brought with her all that her striking and fascinating personality commanded. These were the days when Sandhill Park was the scene of life and activity such as it had not known before nor has since. Then the stables were full of horses, and there was much coming and going and the grass had no time to grow on the coach drive. Then the seats in the Church occupied by the family and the establishment were full on Sundays. Thus eight years passed when the untimely death of the beautiful mistress of the house saw it once more occupied by others. Sir Wroth in due course married his second wife, Gertrude Elizabeth, daughter of the Rev. Charles Theodore Mayo, of Uxbridge.

It is worth alone a visit to Sandhill to see the bust of Anne Williams, now spoken of as the first Lady Lethbridge, which stands in the library, and as you look at the graceful form and beautiful features you will sympathise with the lady to whose lot it fell to fill her place.

There is no portrait or bust that I have seen to give any idea of the second Lady Lethbridge. It must have been a sore trial to her after her marriage to have to wait for the day when she should become mistress of Sandhill Park; to look out from the little low house of Ballifants with longing aspirations upon

the stately pile upon the hill. She had not long to
wait, however. The day came, but it was a sad
home-coming. Married in 1889, in 1890 the second
Lady Lethbridge was brought to Sandhill to be
buried. And now the spirit of Sir Wroth was broken;
he never returned to Sandhill, but retired to end his
days at the Royal Yacht Club at Cowes. We are
said to inherit from our grandparents rather than
from our parents, but Sir Wroth had no taste for
politics. He was a sportsman. The names Newmarket and Everley suggest the turf rather than the
hustings as the bent of his favourite pursuit. At the
former he found a house to his liking, and at the
latter a congenial spirit in his cousin, Sir John
Astley. He died on 26th December, 1902, and was
buried in Ash Priors Churchyard under the shadow of
the Church which he restored.

"On Monday, December 1st, took place the funeral
of the late Sir Wroth Acland Lethbridge at Ash
Priors, and despite the torrents of rain which fell
there was a large attendance of gentry and tenantry,
and the signs of genuine mourning were eloquent
testimony of the general feeling that the late Sir
Wroth was one of the kindliest and most courteous
of men. The opinion was on all hands expressed
that through his death the world was poorer by the
loss of one who was a typical English gentleman of
the old school, a race fast disappearing from our
midst. The body was brought from Cowes, where he
died, by rail as far as Yeovil and thence by road.
The service, which was of a very simple character, was conducted by the Rev. A. E. Baynham,
Vicar of Cothelstone, and the deceased was interred in a brick grave at the western end of the

Churchyard. The grave, which is situated between those of his two wives, was lined with ivy, and the coffin, which was of massive oak, with a shell of elm and leaden casket, was borne upon a bier, employees on the estate acting as bearers." * Those who knew him best would tell you that his noble presence and features corresponded with the largeness of his heart. Not a beggar upon the road but who received assistance from him. His presence on the bench of Magistrates was a guarantee to the prisoner at the bar that if he received his due it would be tempered with mercy. The brass plate was thus inscribed:—

"WROTH ACLAND LETHBRIDGE,
4th Baronet,
Died 26 December, 1902,
Aged 71."

THE LETHBRIDGE ARMS.

Argent over water proper, a bridge of five arches, embattled gules, and over the centre arch a turret in chief, an eagle displayed, sable, charged on the breast with a bezant— My hope is in God.

The crest is an eagle. Motto, "Truth."

The history of a great house will always contain many thrilling episodes, and if the stories which are recorded are not the best that could be told, it is from lack of opportunity of hearing them which is afforded in conversation with those with whom we have had a longer or more intimate acquaintance. We should read of postillions urging on steaming horses and a rumbling coach, in the hurried flight of a happy couple to a small village on the borders of Scotland, in Dumfriesshire, remarkable for the clandestine marriages that

---

* *The Somerset County Gazette.*

until a few years ago were celebrated there by an
officiating blacksmith ; and a still more startling story
of a noble Baronet being pushed into a hearse before
his time by a clever device of his butler to save him
from a too warm reception from his political opponents.

Interesting as these tales may be, and part of the
family history, we turn to better things. It will be
noted that the family crest is an eagle. In the beautiful
window in Bishops Lydeard Church dedicated by
Sir Wroth Periam Christopher Lethbridge to the Glory
of God and in memory of his grandfather, Sir John
Hesketh Lethbridge and his father, Sir Wroth Acland
Lethbridge, the central figure is that of St. John the
Evangelist with the pen with which he was transcribing
part of the Gospel. " The eagle at the feet is always
indicative of that apostle who, through his life lived
for the Lord Jesus Christ, was permitted to such
understanding of the deep mysteries of God." * The
eagle soars above the things of this world and through
the mists which envelop this earth fixes its keen
strong eye undazed by the noon-day sun, thus
suggesting the spirit which prompted the building of a
south aisle to the Church and a school that the children
might be taught the great truths contained in the
Holy Bible and thereby become good Christians and
good subjects, and further to the special work of the
fourth Baronet, Sir Wroth Acland Lethbridge in the
restoration of the Church testifying to a faith which
amidst a goodly heritage and fair surroundings was
to them " the substance of things hoped for, the
evidence of things not seen."   On the left hand of

---

* Quotation from the Bishop's sermon at the unveiling
ceremony.

the window is the figure of King Alfred, which indicates
" the association of the Lethbridge family with that
King. King Alfred was not only the defender of the
people who were committed to his charge, but he used
his splendid opportunities for teaching all his people
what God would have them be." I had not the
honour of knowing either of the ancestors of the
present Baronet, but if you ask me to describe them,
I should do so from the portraits of them which hang
upon the walls of Sandhill Park which impress me
with the idea of remarkable presence and noble features,
and I should say that they were all men of great
stature. " Each one resembled the children of a
King."* In the third light of the window is the figure
of St. Christopher with the figure of Christ upon his
shoulder, from which legend, happily suggested by the
name of the present Baronet and the giver of the
window, we are reminded that we may devote our
physical strength as well as our mental insight to the
service of God and in so doing find it easier than the
service of any other master as we cross the flood,
each using the strength which God has given him
and the gifts with which God has endowed him. The
legend of St. Christopher may not be known to many
of those who will read this account so that it will
not be out of place if I give it here.

It was usual in former times to have a picture of
St. Christopher upon the north wall of the parish
church which, when the entrance was upon the south
side, would be the first object that met the eye of those
who entered the church. The traveller uttered a prayer
before the picture, for this act protected him during
the day from the various dangers of the road.

* Judges viii, 18.

THE LEGEND OF ST. CHRISTOPHER.

There are several versions of the legend of St. Christopher, which, though they differ in detail, agree on the main points, viz., that he was a man of great size and strength, who determined that he would be the subject of none but the mightiest of sovereigns, forasmuch as the lord of such a vassal ought to own no one as his superior, but that if the prince and ruler of all nations were to be discovered anywhere, to him he would devote his service and spend his life in doing his bidding. Offerus, for this was his name, went forth to look for such a master. One day he came to a river by the side of which dwelt a hermit to whom he confided his resolve; but, who was the strongest, the bravest and the best? The hermit told him that he was the Son of Mary. Who is this Son of Mary? asked Offerus. The hermit then advised him to build a hut by the river and devote his great strength to carrying pilgrims across it who wished to worship at a certain shrine, and thus he would be doing a good work and get an answer to his question. One cold starlight night Offerus was asleep when he heard his name being called by a child; he opened his door, but could see nothing. A second time his name was called, and on opening the door he saw before him a beautiful boy who besought him to carry him across the river. Offerus did so, but not without difficulty, for the boy was heavy and the stream was strong. The boy thanked him for his pains and disappeared. Shortly afterwards Offerus was lying ill and sad in his hut, when an angel appeared to him and said that henceforward he should be called Christopher as he had borne Christ. A few days later another angel came and bore

him from his little hut to the palace of the great
King, who, when he saw him, spake to him and said,
" Inasmuch as you have done it unto one of the least
of these my brethren, you have done it unto Me." The
meaning of the word Christopher is Christ bearer.

The window in Ash Priors Church in memory of
Sir Wroth Acland Lethbridge has in the centre light
the figure of our Lord as "the Light of the World,"
after the famous picture by Holman Hunt. On either
side in the other two lights are the figures of SS. Peter
and Paul, to which two Apostles the Priory of Taunton
was dedicated—a reference to the former connection of
Ash Priors Church with Taunton Priory.

St. Peter holds in his hand the keys (St. Matt. xvi.,
19); St. Paul the sword and the book, from his own
illustration, " The sword of the Spirit, which is the
word of God " (Eph. vi., 17.)   In the three spaces
beneath are three shields with the arms of the three
families—Wroth, Acland, Lethbridge—and their mottoes,
" Fide sed cui vide "—" Inebranlable "—" Spes mea in
Deo." In the tracery above are the Alpha and Omega,
and on either side scrolls bearing the mottoes, " Nemo
nisi nomen " and "ὀψὲ θεῶν ἀλέουσι μύλοι ἀλέουσι δὲ λεπτὰ."
(The mill stones of the gods grind late, but they grind
small.)

In the canopies over the centre figure is the sacred
heart representative of love and charity. Over St. Peter
is a model of a church taken from the Priory Seal, and
over St. Paul the open Bible, indicative of " Truth," the
motto of the Lethbridge family.

The window was designed by Sir Wroth G. C.
Lethbridge and the Vicar, with the help of the artist,
Mr. Herbert Davis, of North Finchley, by whom the
beautiful designs were executed.

THE GLEBE FARMS.

THE acquisition of two small farms, the gift of Queen Anne's Bounty to the benefice, has already been mentioned. Queen Anne's Bounty is the name applied to a perpetual fund formed by the surrender to the Church by Queen Anne, with the consent of Parliament, of the first fruits and tenths annexed to the Crown by Henry VIII. for augmentation of the livings of the poorer Anglican Clergy. Annates and decimæ formed originally part of the revenue paid by the Clergy to the Papal exchequer. The former consist of the first whole year's income of all spiritual preferments, the latter of one-tenth of their annual profits after the first year. Benefices under the annual value of £50 are now exempted from the tax.

The farm at Skilgate is known as "Yeanover." It has the disadvantage of being about 15 miles from Ash Priors. The route to Skilgate affords a tiresome though by no means uninteresting ride through Halse, Fitzhead, and Wiveliscombe, thence by very hilly and beautiful scenery through Waterow on the Bampton road as far as Pitton Cross.

When I visited Yeanover Farm with the Diocesan Surveyor it presented a melancholy appearance. The barn was in ruins, the house, which is a fair sized cottage, had been saved by the good slate roof. It has an old-fashioned outside round chimney in front. The one room on the ground floor has an open hearth

in which you may sit and watch the smoke ascend
the chimney. The house internally was getting into
a terrible state and was hardly habitable, but the
farmer and his family, though living in so dilapidated
a house, did not appear to have an empty larder. The
good lady entertained us hospitably with bread and
milk and Devonshire cream. The shepherd dog lay
on the hearth, but refused to take anything from our
hands. "He will not take it from you," said the
farmer, "but if you will give it to me he will eat
it." The dog at once took it from his master's hand.
The bedroom windows are on a level with the floor.
The quaint old oak settle, with a bacon cupboard at
the back, was in keeping with the house. The massive
oak beams had been whitewashed. It was early spring
and the hedgerows were full of primroses and the
gorse in full bloom, such bloom as only to be seen
down in the West of England.* Water was bubbling
up from the ground, falling in cascades and rushing
in every direction. A storm was brewing, heavy
thunder clouds were gathering; down came the rain
as we made for Morebath Station. A wild part of the
country, truly, and yet sought out and selected by
those who live in the Metropolis. And we passed at
least one modern mansion built by Mr. Harrod, and
so in spite of rough roads and drenching rain, and the
somewhat depressing evidence of the rural exodus in-
dicated by empty cottages, dilapidated farm buildings,
and no rent, we had met with hospitality, we had
seen beautiful things, and the recollections left on the
mind were pleasing. The Glebe Farms at both of

---

* The Mountain Ash with its bright red berries grows in
a hedge on the farm, and the yellow mountain poppy in the
lanes.

these places have now been put into thorough repair.
The Rev. V. C. Day writes to say how he did the same
when he first became Vicar of Ash Priors.   He says :—
" When I came to Ash Priors in 1855 I spent, as my
predecessor had nothing, more than £130 on the Skilgate property and the cottages at Kittisford.   I put
the house at Skilgate in thorough repair, a new slate
roof and floorings, in fact everything necessary for the
comfort of the tenant, and since then much has been
laid out.   Since Atkins became the tenant I put new
gates throughout the farm, and also allowed him money
for the internal arrangements of the house.   Whether
the money was really applied to the purpose for which
it was intended I could not say.   The cottages at
Kittisford were of no use, for they were frequently
unoccupied and chiefly built of mud and straw, and a
constant expense to the incumbent.   I took the present
tenant of Yeanover, as his was the only offer of £28.
The other offer was only £20, and the tithes to be
paid by landlord, which would have reduced it to £15,
so that I had no choice."

When I came into the benefice in 1903 the dilapidations were estimated by the Diocesan Surveyor at
£186; Yeanover, £180; Kittisford, £6.   To meet this
heavy amount the Governors of Queen Anne's Bounty
gave a grant of £93 to the benefice on 12th May, 1904.
The dilapidations were contracted for, and the repairs
carried out.   Yeanover Farm was valued at £575
before the repairs were carried out, with a view to
the proposed sale of the farm, but a purchaser prepared to give the amount required to yield an equiva-
lent to the rent was not found.   In addition to the
estimated repairs at Skilgate there were several extra
improvements made, including a new boiler and spouting

round the house. The orchard was replanted with apple trees.

The tithe apportionment of the Skilgate glebe lands is £5 10s. 10d.; tithe rent charge, £3 17s., paid by the Vicar. Of the previous history of Yeanover Farm the present occupier tells me "For a few years prior to 1839 the farm was occupied by Mr. William Bidgood, and in March, 1839, by my grandfather, Mr. John Palmer, who died in 1853, and was then taken over by his widow, Mary Palmer, till her death in 1867, when their son, Mr. Thomas Palmer, took it on till his death in 1889, when I (as his executor) held it till March, 1890, making 51 years in the Palmer family. Mr. William Atkins then took it and held it till 1904, when I took it from you. I think about 40 years ago (or nearly) a new slate roof was put on the house. Before that it was thatched, and just before they took off the old roof my cousin, the late Mr. William Bidgood (for many years Curator of Taunton Museum, and a grandson of the former tenant), made a sketch of the house and painted it. That picture is now in the possession of his widow, Mrs. Bidgood, Old Priory House, St. James' Street, Taunton. An old man I have had a talk with says that a tenant before Mr. Bidgood, he has heard, was Mr. James Hill, but he cannot remember him and does not know if he was next before Mr. Bidgood."

The property at Kittisford was purchased in 1738 by the Governors from Thomas Wright, of Wiveliscombe, who purchased it in 1737 from Matthew Haviland, of Langford Budville, and the property at Skilgate was purchased in 1793 from Andrew Hill, of Skilgate.

The Local Commissioners, who reported on the property at Skilgate in 1791, stated that it was liable to a payment of 1s. 3d. per annum (called "Queen's Dowry") to Miss Acland, lady of the manor.

The manor of Skilgate was granted to John Leigh, Esq., by Henry VIII. as parcel of the estates of the monastery of Abbotsbury, Dorset, by the heiress of whose descendant, Sir John Leigh, Knight, it came to the family of Fitzgarrat, and is now the property of Lady Acland. Agnes Leigh, daughter of Sir John Leigh, Knight, as has already been mentioned, married Edward Fitzgarrat, and the Manor and Rectory of Ash Priors was granted by Henry VIII. to John Leigh, Esq., from whom it descended to the present owners, the Lethbridges, so that it appears that the Manor of Skilgate was originally the property of the same family which owned the Manor of Ash Priors.

Yeanover, a curious name, sometimes spelt Yend-over, sometimes Hendover, but wrongly I think. I expect this is not the original name of the farm. It was probably called after someone who owned it or had held it in years gone by, but it came to be called Yeanover. There were two fields adjoining one another on the slope of the hill; No. 61 on the tithe map was called " Square Piece," and No. 62, Yonder Cleave. Now these two fields have been merged into one by the removal of the partition, faint traces of which may still be seen, and the one large field is known as Yonder Cleave, the cleave over yonder, of course, and it is easy to understand how it came to be known as Yendover, and so to give the name to the whole farm Yeanover. There were originally three orchards, but the trees have died and been cut down. They were called respectively No. 65, Home Orchard; No. 66, Back Orchard; and No. 69, Bottom Orchard; No. 51 is called Water Leat Meadow; No. 63, Home

Yeanover Farm.

Cleave; No. 52, Ball Cleave; No. 67, Gratton; No. 68, Bottom Piece; No. 59, Great Longland; No. 60, Little Longland; No. 58, Luckham; No. 12, Paddock; No. 50, Home Meadow. The house formerly had another ground floor room, but this room got into a bad state and was pulled down.

Kittisford is nearer home, half a day's journey there and back. The route to this place by road is through Halse, Milverton, Langford Budville and Wellisford. The glebe fields lie on the left hand, on the slope of the hill, a little beyond a house called Kittisford Villa. The present tenant has occupied the land as far back as the days when Mr. Lawrence was Vicar of Ash Priors. Mr. F. Hayman is the owner of Kittisford Mills, which lie on the right, a short distance after the turning to Greenham and Ashbrittle. The journey is a tiresome one, there being many hills, but the return journey is more quickly accomplished; from Langford Church it is down hill most of the way. On the glebe land there were two cottages, the site of which was marked by two heaps of stones. These by the Bishop's order have been cleared away and removed from the plan, and the three fields have been thrown into one.

SALE OF GLEBE LAND.

By a formal instrument of consent to accept £150, the produce of glebe land sold in the year 1831, dated 11 Dec., 1889, the Governors of Q.A.B. received from the Rev. Vaughan C. Day, Vicar of Ash Priors, £150 upon trust to lay out and invest the same in the public funds of Great Britain and to pay the dividends and produce of such investment as and when the same shall become due and be received, to the Vicar for the time being of the Vicarage of Ash Priors; the income received is upon the stock purchased, viz., £154 12s. 9d. The sealed deed is in the iron safe.

This sum was derived from the sale of a small portion of glebe situated in the parish of Kittisford to the Great Western Canal Company in 1831. It was subsequently sold to the Great Western Railway Company at the time of the construction of the line. The area of the land is not mentioned.

ASH PRIORS WORTHIES.

IT only requires a little imagination to recall the
days of 878, when King Alfred was collecting
his army at Athelney and the manhood of the
village setting out in obedience to the summons of
the King to meet the dreaded Danes at Ethandun ; or
later on when in 1685 the Duke of Monmouth chose
Somersetshire as the scene of his attempt to overthrow
James II., and his standard waved over Taunton
Castle, where twenty young maids of rank, led by Miss
Sarah Blake with sword in one hand and book in
the other, presented him with colours of their handi-
work, together with a copy of the Bible. And we can
picture to ourselves troops of horsemen from the West
Country galloping across Ash Common on their way
to fight on the fatal field of Sedgemoor. It is a mere
inference drawn from the fact of their absence from
home at the time that three men, named Gabriel
Street, William Hall, and Robert Nation, from Ash
Priors, took part in the Monmouth rebellion. Which
side they took is, of course, equally uncertain, but
there is reason to believe that one of them at least
took up arms against the King. An extract from the
London Gazette, No. 2120, 15th March, 1685, concerning Gabriel Spratt, of Ash Priors, describes him as
" excepted from the general pardon " proclaimed on
10th March.

They are all three described in the original manuscript

in the British Museum as husbandmen belonging
to Ash Priors. The name Gabriel seems to have been
common at that time if Streete is not a misprint for
Spratt. The name Hall is of constant occurrence,
and Hill may be seen on the tombstones. It is the
same name spelt differently. Robert Nation is the only
one of the three that can be identified. His name
was upon the 5th bell as church warden in 1686,
which exactly corresponds with the date of the rebellion.
The precise transcript of the names of the Ash
Priors people referred to in Add. MSS. 30,077 and
28ª is :—

Ashpryors.

Gabriel Streete, de Ashpryors, husbandman	Absent from
Willus Hull, de Eadem, husbandman	their homes
Robtus Nation, de Eadem, husbandman	in the tyme
P. Willm Gifford, Const. prdto.	of the Re-
	bellion.

It is a curious fact that in the *London Gazette* for
15th March, 1685, the name Gabriel Spratt is given,
but in the manuscript we are now speaking of Gabriel
Streete is mentioned. Which it was, or whether they
were one and the same person, we cannot possibly say;
but it is interesting to find that both Spratt and Street
are still local names. Hull, Hill and Hall were
always interchangeable names. The village which we
now know as Bishops Hull is almost always, in old
days, referred to as Hill Bishops. The name of the
constable also appears in the register; Sarah Gifford,
infant, was buried 16th Nov., 1794.

Now, though I do not find the name Spratt at
all, the fact that Elizabeth Street obtained a settlement
in the parish in the year 1682 would seem to point
to the fact that she either had relations in Ash Priors

or that her family had been associated with it at some time.

Whereas Elizabeth Street of the pish of Staplefitzpain in the county of Somerset, spinster, for her better livelyhood is desirous by your permission and leave to come into your pish of Ashpriars in the county aforesaid there to live and make her abode now for the furtherance thereof wee whose names are subscribed the Minister churchwardens and overseers for the poore of the said pish of Staplefitzpaine doe for our selves and our purressions Minister churchwardens and overseers for the poore and for the rest of our said pish of Staplefitzpaine do covenant promise and agree with you the Minister churchwardens and overseers for the poore and the rest of your said pish of Ashpriars that if the said Elizabeth Street shall or may by poverty or any way or means there to become chargeable or any way burthensome unto your said pish of Ashpriars thenupon notice thereof unto us or our successors wee will receive and take back again the said Elizabeth Street into our said pish of Staplefitzpain and free and discharge you of and from the burthen and charge of her for witnesse whereof wee have hereunto set our hands and seals the eight and twentyth day of October and in thirty fourth year of the reign of our Soveraign Lord King Charles the Second by the grace of God over England and in the year of our Lord 1682.

> Robt. Axe Rector
> Witt. Axe and Steeven Turner Churchwardens
> Rob. Dyke
> The mark of   } Overseers
> Tristram X Huet

By the will of Nicholas Streate, of Bridgwater, dated 1st Nov., 1616, and proved by Mary his relict, part of the Manor of Ash Priors, Somerset, is bequeathed to his second son, Edward Streate (*Somerset Wills*, Vol. I., 63).

We are told that when Monmouth landed at Lyme Regis, in Dorsetshire, he commissioned Sir John Trenchard to raise a troop in Taunton, but that he failed to enlist a sufficient number of men, hence if the Taunton men afterwards flocked to Monmouth's standard, it was rather under compulsion than of their own free will.   This fact may have helped to contribute towards the issue of a proclamation of pardon by the King, to which, however, some exceptions were made.   One man who was probably willing to join the troop was Gabriel Spratt, of Ash Priors.   What he actually did we are not told, only that he was one of those who was not pardoned, and we are left to imagine his fate.   What must have been the feelings of the people of Ash Priors at that time is easily realized when under Judge Jeffreys the rigour of the law exceeded the military tyranny under Colonel Kirke, how the women and children would wait at their doors to hear the reports brought home by their husbands and fathers from Taunton, of executions on the Cornhill, among whom might hang the body of the ill-fated Gabriel Spratt.   There is no trace of the family left in the village, nor mention of the name in the registers, but the name still exists in the parish of Fitzhead.

Pyleigh, a farm, the extent of which is estimated in the valuation list of the parish at 28a. or. 14p., and also as the gift of Jordan de Molton to the Priory of Taunton, has an historic interest in having been at one time the property of the Vane family.

When in the reign of Charles II. an act of pardon and indemnity was passed, a special exception was made of those who had directly and personally taken part in the murder of the late King.   Lambert and Vane had been excepted from the general pardon and committed to prison.   Hume tells that the indictment of Vane did not comprehend any of his actions during the war between the King and Parliament; it extended

only to his behaviour after the King's death, as member
of the Council of State and Secretary of the Navy,
where fidelity to the trust imposed in him required his
opposition to monarchy.   Vane wanted neither courage
nor capacity to avail himself of this advantage.   He
pleaded the famous statute of Henry VII., in which
it was enacted that no man should ever be
questioned for his obedience to the King de facto;
urged that whether the established government
were a monarchy or a commonwealth, the reason
of the King was still the same, and maintained that
the Commons were the root and foundation of all lawful
authority.   But this bold defence only hastened his
destruction, and he was executed on 14 June, 1662.
Vane's courage did not desert him when condemned,
and lest pity for a brave sufferer should make impression on the populace, drummers were placed under
the scaffold to drown his voice when he attempted
to address the people.

At any rate Ash Priors is connected with one
man of world-wide fame whose brilliant achievements
proudly sustained the honour of this country and greatly
enhanced its naval character.   Among his numerous
gallant exploits the most noted are the four desperate
engagements fought with the Dutch fleet under Admiral
Van Tromp, by which he not only gained a decided
superiority over our mightiest naval opponent, but by
the bold tactics he introduced, infused that intrepidity
and spirit of enterprise by which the British Navy has
been ever since so highly distinguished.

Mr. Humphreys writes, " I am not acquainted with
any publication or any source of information that
would enable you to trace the connection of the Blakes
with Ash Priors.   One knows that certain members

of the Blake family lived there, and I believe Admiral Blake's family originally came from Ash Priors, although he himself was born at Bridgwater." In the adjoining parish of Halse there are two houses called after the family Upper and Lower Blakes. In Ash Priors, where the family are known to have lived, nothing remains of them but their tombstone.

We should be glad if we could trace the connection, and it would be interesting to know where they lived. The arms of the family are *argent a chevron between three garbs sable*. Though the Blakes were the oldest family connected with the place that we can trace they do not appear ever to have been Lords of the Manor.

ACTION OF ROGER SEMSON AGAINST JOHN TILER, TEMP. QUEEN ELIZABETH.

We have abundant authority for the claim which Ash Priors lays to the famous bell-founder, Roger Semson, as a parishioner, but where he lived is not known and not a trace of his foundry remains. Tradition, which is always valuable, locates it somewhere at the south west of the Priory and between it and the road which runs across the Common. It was somewhere back as far as the year 1548. It is a mere conjecture that he may have lived at the Priory. That he was a man possessed of some property, although he did not manage his affairs very wisely, is shown by the following action in the Court of Chancery brought by him against John Tyler in the year 1558 or thereabouts. The bell-founder appears to have fallen upon evil times, and to have been reduced to the necessity of raising money upon the security of his tenement and 10 acres, the lease of which he had for 99 years.

It affords an illustration of Roger Semson's position, and of the English of the period, and serves as a wholesome warning to his successors not to entangle themselves with money lenders. Roger Semson's actions betray an amount of simplicity which seems to justify his modest opinion of himself when he describes himself as " a poor, aged, impotent and unlettered person," setting his seal to documents concerning which he admits "what they contain I know not."

To the righte honourable Sir Nicholas Baker, Knight, Lord Keeper of the Great Seale of England.

Most lamentablie complaynethe unto your honourable Lordshippe youre poore and daylie orator Roger Symson of Ash Priors in the Co. Somerset Bell-founder that whereas your Lordship's s^d poore Orator is lawfully seised of one tenement in Ashepriors during the widowhood of Agnes Langman of Ashepriors and whereas your poor Orator bought a lease in reversion of the s^d tenement and ten acres of land belonging to Sir John Alic, Knight decessed for 99 years and whereas your Lordshipp's s^d poore Orator being occasioned thereunto for his necessarie use borrowed of one of his neighbours called Thomas Pyle £12 and gave unto the said Thomas Pyle the said writings and lease to gage and pawne for the more sure paiement of the same. So it is. And it maie please your good Lordship that one John Taylor of Stokegumber husband man being a man of verie lewde and craftie condition as hereafter in some sort shall appeare, understanding that your same poore orator had pawned the lease of the premesses as aforesaid came unto the said Thomas Pile most earnestlye cravinge that the s^d Thomas Pile would deliver unto him your Lordshippes poore orator's said lease upon paiment by him of the s^d £12 which he the s^d Thomas Pile utterly refused to doe with-out the consent of your Lordshippes s^d poore orator which the said John Tyler perceiving he could not other wise attayne to his evil purpose and synister meaning by divers craftie and subtle means sought for and at length obteigned so as the s^d John Tyler paieing unto the s^d Thomas Pile the £12 your Lordships s^d poor orator became indebted unto him for the same, and by marvellous deceitful invensions and craftie practices the said John Tiler hath sithens moste fraudulentlie and craftelie procured your Lordshippes s^d poore Orator Partlie by colour that he was indebted unto him in the s^d somme of £12 and partlie by reason that a little before he John Tiler had likewise craftelie and subtellie caused your Lordship's poor orator to be bounden unto him for the paiement of £17.

John Tiler's Defence.

John Tiler's reply to the charges brought against him shows that Semson became indebted to him for £17 and gave a bond for £36 for its repayment at certain dates, but did not pay it. Semson also owed £12 to Thomas Pile and had given the lease in mortgage of his tenement, which was like to be lost, had not I saved the case. I paid Thomas Pile his £12. Semson on Nov. 4, xi. Queen Elizabeth, made over all his title to the tenement and also a bond for £10, the lease not being worth the £30 due to me. Semson paid the £10 and received the bond back while I entered into the tenement, the £20 not being paid.

Semson's Reply to Tiler.

He says that about four years ago Tiler being verie evill and craftelie minded came to my house at Ashepriors to entreate with him for the marriage of one of my daughters unto one George Parker faith fullie protesting that Parker was a substantial and wealthie person who owed no man anything except 20/- to Tiler, the day of payment of which was not yet due. Accordingly Semson concluded a marriage between his daughter and Parker. Parker afterwards offered the 20 shillings to Tiler, but Tiler asked him and Semson, his father-in-law, to come to his house at Stokegoummer, which they did. In his house he told Semson, the father-in-law, that Parker owed him £17, of which he had the greatest need, and to avoid vexation, trouble and expenses to Parker, Tiler craftilie and subtelie persuaded and enticed Semson to enter into the said bond of £36.   Tiler, in a lengthy reply, denies everything that Semson had said about Parker.

The appeal of John Howe, to the High Court of Chancery, for the recovery of his title deed to 40 acres of Land in Ash Priors, in the Reign of Queen Elizabeth (1588).

In most humble wise complayninge sheweth unto youre good Lordshipp your poore and daylie Orator John Howe of Aish Pryors yeoman that whereas Sir John Lee Knight, in the Lief tyme was lawfullie seased of the manor of Aishpriors, and about 26 years ago at a Courte holden in the said manor by his Steward and Surveyor of the same manor did grant by copie of Courte Roll according to the custom of the said manor unto one John Wrentmore father-in-lawe unto your said orator for term of their lives and of the longest living, one tenement containing 40 acres of arable land, meadow and pasture, in Aishepriors.   And about 10 years ago John Wrentmore died, your Orator being then 10 years of age. And then Barbara wife of the said John Wrentmore engaged the same during her widowhood according to the custom of the said manor and after married and toke to husband one John Furse by means whereof the said tenement descended unto your orator by reason of the grant of the copy aforesaid and then the said John Furse desired the friends of your said Orator that he might occupie the same tenement until such time as your said Orator should accomplish the age of 21 yeares promising his friends that he would yield it unto him at that time such sums of money as the tenement should be worth above the Lord's rente and that he would also repair and maintain the said tenement and houses, hedges and ditches.   So it is moste gracious Lorde that the said John Furse having no interest nor title to the same tenement but of trust committed to the use of your said orator occupied it for 10 years being worth yearlie above the lorde's rente 16

pounds and never paid anything for the same. And he hath
spoiled and wasted the houses and hedges of the same to
the hinderance of your said orator of 20 pounds and also
withholdeth the copie of court roll granted unto the same
John Wrentmore and your said Orator to the utter undoing of
your said Orator for ever unless your good lordship's aide
moved with pitie be to him extended in this behalfe. In tender
consideration whereof and forasmuch as your said orator
hathe diverse and sundrie tymes gently required and desired
the said John Furse to yeld to him an account of the profittes
of the same premisses and to deliver unto him his said copie
of courte roll yet notwithstandinge he hath at all tymes hitherto
refused and denied the same and yet doth contrarie to all
lawe refuse equitie and good conscience. May it therefore
please your good lordship to grant unto your said Orator the
Queen's Majesties gracious writ of suppoena to be directed
unto the said John Furse commanding him by virtue thereof
to be and personally appear before your good lordship in the
Queen's Majesties high Court of Channcerie at a certain daie
and under a certain payne to answer to the premises.

PRIVATE JOHN DAVIS, OF THE COLDSTREAM GUARDS.

To give everyone their due the parish of Tolland
has the honour of having produced this worthy man.
I am not quite sure, but I think he must have fought
at Waterloo, and that is how he came to be discharged
as disabled about the year 1819. Born, as he believed,
in that parish about the year 1780, he entered the
army in 1797, and after serving for 23 years in the
army, he retired on a pension of 6d. a day. He appears
to have wished to obtain a settlement in Ash Priors,
in which parish he had once lived for a year in the
service of Miss Nancy Hill for his victuals, for which
purpose he underwent an examination before Mr. M.
Blake, J.P., on the 9th Feb., 1820. He appears to
have remembered a good deal of his past history, but
was not quite sure of the place of his birth or of his

dates. But one thing of which he had a distinct recollection was a certain second-hand coat and waistcoat which he got for his pains when he was a lad in the service of the late Mrs. Allen, bankrupt, of Tolland Mills.

Tolland has been mentioned before as having been visited by the Vicar of Ash Priors. There was another family of some importance in the parish of Ash Priors which hailed from Tolland. Samuel Woolcott and Henry, who succeeded him as Churchwarden, were both in service at Sandhill Park, the latter being steward on the estate. They lived at Ballifants, and trace their descent from the old Somersetshire family of Woolcotts whose home was in the parish of Tolland. In the churchyard of that parish may be seen the old tomb with inscription scarcely legible:

Here lieth the body of John Woolcot, 21, March, 1618. Here also lieth the body of Johne Woolcot, mother of the said John Woolcot, who died the 5th of April, 1637.

Mr. Isaac Blackmore, late private in the Coldstream Guards, a native of Ash Priors, enlisted in the army in the year 1847; he served in the Crimean War, being present in the engagements of Alma, Inkerman, Balaclava and at the siege of Sebastapol, for which he received the medal and clasp, and also one for long service and good conduct. He witnessed the charge of the Light Brigade, being in the front line. The Turks, who should have covered their retreat, spiked their guns and deserted them. The guns were retaken by the Coldstream Guards. This Crimean veteran came of a family of twelve.

Ash Priors is rather conspicuous for small families, not so in former years. In the cottage which was afterwards enlarged to make what is known as Rock

House and is now the Vicarage, Sarah Burcher was the mother of eleven children. Seven of her sons entered the army. The Burchers appear to have lived long lives as well as had long families. Mary Burcher's name appears in the burial register, 5 March, 1854, aged 99 years.

Ash Priors supplied its contingent to the late South African War of 1901-2, both in the Artillery and Infantry. J. Warren, R.A., was called up from the Reserves and went through the campaign, for which he received medal and clasps.

John House, though a young man, is an old soldier. He served in India in the Black Mountain and Hazara Expeditions, for which he received the Indian Frontier medal and clasps. From India he went to South Africa and fought his way with the Royal Welsh Fusiliers from the Tugela to Ladysmith, which he describes as one long battle in which every inch of the way was stubbornly contested. In spite of the risks to which he was thus exposed and the sickness which he contracted, he nevertheless returned home to engage in more peaceful occupations.

At the north-west corner of the Common, adjoining the Priory Cottages, there stood a small farmhouse which has disappeared, and the barn has been converted into cottages. This farm was occupied for many years by a worthy old couple named William and Mary Langdon—brother and sister. They do not, however, appear to have been very successful in farming, for they had to come on the parish.

Old William was the first to go. "How could the poor old man live when his sister, out of sheer kindness of her heart, would insist upon his eating bread and cheese when he was dying." Mary Langdon only survived her brother a short while. Adverse circumstances, followed by the loss of her brother, preyed on her mind, and toward the end she became mentally as well as bodily infirm and died leaving what little property she still possessed to Sir Wroth Lethbridge, on condition that he should pay her funeral expenses and keep up the grave. It is still remembered in the parish how Sir Wroth, with characteristic good nature and sympathy for the poor, attended her funeral.

The late tenant of Court Farm, Mr. John Blackmore, is deserving of mention as having worked his way up in life by his own industry. Though not a native of Ash Priors he came into the parish as a working man and in time he was in a position to rent the principal farm in the parish. Owing to some disagreement between himself and his landlord he received notice to quit the farm. He died before the notice expired. Whilst his landlord had been selling one piece of his property after another, he had been accumulating a very considerable fortune.

COPIES OF CERTAIN OLD FORMS OF DISCHARGE, AND SETTLEMENT, INDENTURES OF APPRENTICESHIP, EXAMINATION OF CASES, AND PERSONS.

In reading them we are struck with the importance of the Churchwarden and Overseer of the poor. They were second only to the Justices of the Peace, and their legal appointment would be carefully watched when " each parish was always squabbling with its neighbours as to which poor belonged to which." The Overseers of the poor owe their origin to the state of affairs which

existed about the year 1597, when for the first
time each parish was called upon to nominate
four householders which " shall be called Overseers of the poor." That was because so many
poor persons were starving, that some steps had
to be taken to put a stop to it. The Overseers,
nominated by the ratepayers and appointed by
the Justices, met with the Churchwardens once a
month and decided what sum of money must be
raised to relieve the poor, and to place out as
apprentices the children of those parents who
were not able to maintain them.

THE EXAMINATION OF MARY PEARCE.

Exeter to wit. The Examination of Mary Pearce, wife of
Richard Pearce, mason, apprehended wandering and begging
in the Parish of Saint Mary Major, in the said City, taken
on oath respecting the place of her last legal settlement and
also of her two children.

The said Examinant on her oath saith that she is the
lawful wife of the said Richard Pearce whose settlement, as
she hath heard him say, is in the parish of Ash, in the
county of Somerset, by serving his apprenticeship there, and
that he never to her knowledge did any act to gain any
other settlement, and further that she hath two children by
her said husband, one Elizabeth aged about nine years and
Mary aged about seven months.

Taken on oath this second day of
October, 1790, before me,
B. H. Walker.
} The Mark of
X Mary Pearce.

During Roman Catholic times the poor were
chiefly supported by the abbeys, convents, priories,
and other religious establishments. The dissolution
of the religious houses had the effect of increasing
the number of vagrants and beggars, and diminishing
the means of support which was met by voluntary

contributions, until in the reign of Queen Elizabeth compulsory relief of the poor was established by the introduction of Poorhouses. But this remedy of the evil soon resulted in a new development, ultimately increasing the burden and pauperising the labourers. Labourers' wages were frequently paid in part by compulsory relief, and thus a portion of the farmers' labour was done at the expense of the parish. In 1828 the rates had risen to 10 shillings in the pound. The ratepayers and the overseers were at their wits end. Their chief object was to keep down the poor rate. By the Poor Law Amendment Act in 1834, the system of paying labourers' wages out of the poor rate was abolished and relief was only to be given to able-bodied persons in "the house." Those who had taken advantage of the poorhouse preferred to throw off the mask, and take to the roads again. Thus Mary Pearce found it more profitable wandering and begging in Exeter than living in the poorhouse, which was of course a place for people to work in, or working for her living in Ash Priors.

This Indenture made the fourth day of Aprill in the eight and twentieth yeare of the Raigne of our Sovraigne Lord Kinge Charles the Seacond over England et Anno Dom 1677 Between William Kerswell, Henry Hall, William Nation and John Hiccarry Churchwardens Overseers of the pish. of Ash Priors in the County of Somesett of the one ptie and Robert Blake of the parrish aforesaid Gent of the other ptie Wittnesseth that the said Churchwardens and Overseers by and with the consent of Robertt Granbey and Edwarde Clarke Esqre two of his Majesties Justices of the Peace for the said County have by these presents put and bound out Mary Gobidge a poor childe of the parish afores[d.] an apprentice to and with the said Robert Blake with him the said Robert Blake his exectors Adms. or Assignes to dwell and as a faithful apprentice him or them to serve from the date hearof until she shall attaine unto the full age of one and twenty years accordinge to the forme of the statutes in that behalfe made and provided by and dureinge all which time the said churchwardens and overseers by force and virtue of the same statute doe order and appoynt that the s^d. apprentice her s^d. master his Exectors Admins. and Assignes will and truly shall serve in all things fitt and requisett for such an apprentice . to doe and shall behave herself truly and honestly in word and deed and the s^d. Robert Blake for himself his Exec^t. Admins. and Assignes doth covenant and promise to instructe and bringe up or cause to be instructed and brought up the s^d. Mary Gobidge his s^d. apprentice in housewifery worke and to finde unto his said apprentice sufficiente meate drinke and apparrell and all other things fitt and nessessary dureinge the terme aforesaid and att the end thereof to discharge the aforesaid apprentice well and sufficiently apparrelled in wittness whereof the parties above said to these presents there hands and seals interchangeably have sett the day and year above written sealed and delivered in the presence of

Robt. Blake.

This indenture is of local interest on account of the name Robert Blake. The date which is given as the 28th year of the reign of King Charles II. has a national significance. Charles II. reigned for eighteen years, but by the act of oblivion the period of the Commonwealth is included in his reign, viz., from 1649, when Charles I. was executed, to 1678. The date of this indenture, 1677, makes it exactly 28 years.

THE CASE OF HENRY CREDGE.

SOMS^ETT.

To ye Churchwardens & Ov. seers of the poore of the pish of Milverton these,

Whereas Henry Credge by virtue of a certificate under the hands of the Minister, the then Constable, Churchwardens &

Ovseers of ye poore of your said pish bearinge date ye sixth day of Apprill in ye yeare of our Lord God 1668 came out of your said pish of Milverton into the pish of Ashpriors otherwise Esse priors there to make his abode for his better mainetenance & livelyhood, in which certificate ye said Henry Credge is owned to be a pishoner by the said pish of Milverton and to be received back againe into your said pish of Milverton in case the said Henery Credge through any affliction shall be brought into distresse and neede, and it beinge made aweare unto us that ye said Henry Credge his wife and children who are all very younge and all under the age of seaven yeares and now in greate want and neede and both father & mother & all the said children relieved & mainetained by ye said pish of Ashpriors otherwise Esse Priors. These are therefore in His Majesties name to will and require you to receive him the said Henery Credge his wife and children into your said pish of Milverton and also to provide and maineteine the said Henry Credge and his wife and also to provide and mayteyne all theire children until they shall severilly accomplish and attaine unto the age of seaven yeares beinge until that age in the condition and nature of nursse children and to be by you mayteyned & provided for according to law. Given under our hands and seales this tenth day of October Anno Regni Regis Caroli 2nd Vicessimo Octavo Annoque Dom. 1676.

John Turberville.
Willm Ciarke.

Milverton and Ashbrittle Confirmed.

The certificate referred to from the Overseers of the parish of Milverton, bearing the given date, the 6th April, 1668, is also found in the box, where it has been lying amongst a lot of old papers for the last 239 years, and is still preserved.

Whereas Henry Credge of the parish of Milverton is desierose to travele for his better maineteynance and livelyhood We the Minister Churchwardens and Overseers of the poore of the pish of Milverton doe certify and promise that we doe owne him for our pishioner and that we will at any time hereafter receive back againe the said Henry Credge into our parysh and keep and indemnify and save harmeless any pish where he shalle get on work if through any affliction he shall be brought into distresse and neede. Wittness our hands this sixth day of Aprill in the year of our Lord God one thousand six hundred and sixty eight.

Willm Granger, *Min.*
Gyles King, *Constable.*

The Mark of
William X Preedy } *Church Wardens.*

George Hellings
Robert Bayly } *Ov. Seers.*

It appears from another document that the time came when Mr. Credge wished to return to Milverton. The document showeth that about eight years since and upwards one Henry Credge, of the parish of Milverton, came to reside in the parish of Ash Priors and brought with him a discharge signed by the names of the Minister, Churchwardens, and Overseers of the poor of the parish of Milverton, with a condition therein inserted that they would receive him back again into Milverton if at any time hereafter he should become chargeable. Now about three months since Credge became chargeable to the parish of Ash Priors, whereupon he was by order of Mr. Turberville and Mr. Wm. Clarke returned to Milverton, but the overseers refused to receive him.

Robt. Nation { William Spratt, one of the Overseers, giving as his reason because they went first to the Minister of Milverton and did not come first to him, which if they had done they would have received him.

Wm. Granger {

They allege that the names subscribed are not the proper hand writing of the said parties, and to make it good they have threatened Robert Bayly, one of the Overseers, to make him a public example, &c., &c., if he did own or confess that he had given consent to John Newton to subscribe his name to the said discharge, and by their threatenings procured the said Bayly to subscribe a note to that effect. And to keep the said Bayly from coming to declare the truth of the matter, William Spratt aforesaid told the said Bayly that whereas Mr. Seaman had two actions against him both should be waived if he would not go to Wells.

Notwithstanding all which the said Bayly calling to mind what he had formerly done and upon what condition the said Newton did undertake to execute the said office for him, the said Bayly by a certificate under his hand hath declared that he did give his order and consent to subscribe his name.

Wm. Granger
Robt. Nation. {

And Wm. Pridy, one of the Churchwardens hath owned by a certificate under his hand that the mark in the discharge was set with his own hand.

Wm. Granger {

If they object, it is not George Holling's hand, we answer it was there put by his order.

Robert Bayly, being an unlearned man and being the said Overseer, hired John Newton to do the office for him and gave him for his pains twenty shillings.

Somsett. Ye Record Wells Sess: xxviii Car: Sedi Reg.

Upon reading an order made under the hands and seals of John Turberville and William Clarke Esqres. two of his

Majesties' Justices of the Peace of this County, concerning the
settlement of one Henry Credge with his wife and family and
upon reading a certificate and discharge under the hands of
the minister charchwardens and overseers of the poor of the
parish of Milverton in the said county whereby the parishioners
of Milverton aforesaid declared the said Credge to be their
parishioner, and upon full hearing their difference between
the parishioners of Ash Priors in the said county and the said
parishioners of Milverton concerning the settlement of the
said Credge and what would be allowed by counsel appearing
on the behalf of either said pish. This court doth confirme the
said order made by the aforesaid justices and doth order that
the said Henry Credge with his wife and family be henceforth
absolutely setled within the said pish of Milverton there to be
provided for according to law they being now chargeable to
the pish of Ash Priors aforesaid.

Per Our Examinatum per Oliverum Bennett, jun^{r.}

Deput Clericum, pacis Comitatus predicti.

This is a true coppy of ye originall ⎫ John Wescombe
   order examined by us   ⎬ Abraham Handcocke

The whole affair appears to have been a little
bit of bribery and corruption on the part of the
Overseers of Milverton to get off receiving back
their old friend, Mr. Henry Credge, not very credit-
able to them or complimentary to him.

It was most difficult for people to move out of
their own parish into another. They could not do so
at all without a certificate, and even if a person had
one, the overseers would caution every one not to let
him a house or farm of less than £10 a year
rent, with the hope of keeping him out, for they never
knew when he might come on the parish, so of course
when Henry Credge went to reside at Ash Priors "for
his better maintenance and livelyhood" the overseers
of the poor at Milverton would be quite prepared to

receive him back again, but they were not quite so
ready when the time came.   And it was a strong
point in his favour when John Davis was able to state
upon oath that "he had never rented £10 a year, or
ever done any other act of his belief, whereby to gain
a settlement in any other parish."

It was well for the young men of the parish to be
boarded out and better fed and taught their trade; but
it was little better than slavery, and the agreement
which the simple young boy was made to sign for five
years was a very one-sided affair :—

During which time the said apprentice his master shall
and will serve, his secrets keep, his lawful commands everywhere gladly do. He shall do no damage to his said master
nor see it to be done by others, but to his power shall prevent
or forthwith give notice to his said master of the same. The
goods of his said master he shall not waste, nor the same
without License of him to any give or lend. Hurt to his said
master he shall not do, or cause or procure to be done. He
shall not buy or sell without his master's licence. Taverns or
alehouses he shall not haunt, at cards, dice or any other
unlawful games he shall not play, nor from the service of his
said master day or night absent himself, but in all things as
an honest and faithful apprentice shall and will demesne and
behave himself towards his said master and all his during the
said term.

To such an agreement James Burston, aged about
sixteen, is asked to put his mark against his own name,
wrongly spelt, when, in the year 1793, he was bound
to Mr. John Hill in respect of Ash Wood, Horses
Meadows, Pile's House, and Pitt Closes; Mrs.
Elizabeth Fouracres for part of Durborows, and
Mr. Bryant for part of Durborows to be con-
tributors.

James Burston, probably the son of James Burston,

the miller, was left an orphan by the death of his
father the previous year, and was no doubt none the
healthier for being descended from a father whose
occupation was one of those so injurious to health. I
hope that young James found in Mr. John Hill and
Mr. Bryant kind masters, and a sympathetic mistress
in Mrs. Elizabeth Fouracres; that among her little
store of home-made medicines she found something to
relieve the cough which he found so troublesome in
the cold damp winter days when he went forth to the
faithful discharge of his manifold duties. His five
years' apprenticeship at length expired, and James
Burston was qualified to earn a man's wage if only
his health had admitted of it. But I think his cough
increased, and although he survived till the summer
of the following year, one funeral which wound
up the village street that year was that of James
Burston, who was laid to his rest on the 5th of
July, 1799.

THE WILL OF EDWARD ALVER, OTHERWISE DOLLEN, OF ASHPRYORS, SOMERSET, YEOMAN, PROVED 1655.

I give to Elizabeth Alver, otherwise dollen my mother all
my new corn and graine in barne and in Mowe which was
grown the Harvest now last past, also all my hogges and swine
and all my butter and cheese, unto Henry Alver *alias* dollen
my eldest sonne 10s. at 21, to William my son £20 at 21, if
my overseers shall not lay it out before for the better pre-
ferment of my said son, to Edward Alver my tenement called
Cames Moore in the parish of Bishops Lidiard which I lately
purchased of John Mallett, Esq. I do make my loving friends
Henry and John White of Carden within the said parish of
Ashpryors executors and overseers in witness whereof I have
hereunto set my hand and seal Nov. 14th, 1655, the mark

of Edward Alver otherwise dollen, published and declared in the presence of us

Henry Hadderidge,
William Carswell,
the mark of John Walters.

48 Berkeley.

Upon John Knight's settlement the seals of the three justices of the peace are well preserved, W. H. Dawe, M. W. Dyke and John Sanford, the latter having six martlets, three in the upper right hand and three in the lower left hand corner. The Rev. H. C. Launder pointed them out to me and thus corrected a mistake which I had made in describing the inn at Langford Budville as the Swallow, and attributing it to the arms of the Arundels. The inn is called the Martlet, being the property of the Sanfords of Chipleigh Park. He, however, attributed the swallow-like appearance of the bird to the ignorance of the artist. It appears, on the contrary, that the artist displayed his wisdom in the representation, rather than his ignorance, for the Martlet in heraldry, is a fanciful bird shaped like a Martin or Swallow, but depicted with short tufts of feathers in the place of legs. It is the difference or distinction of a fourth son. If it is intended to represent a real bird, it is the house or Sand Martin. It was formerly written by some authors "Martlet." John Sanford, Esq., was Member of Parliament for Taunton in 1685, in the reign of James II, and also in the Convention Parliament in 1688.

Christophor Brown's indenture is signed and sealed by Edward Clarke, Esq., M.P. for Taunton in 1698, 1701, 1702, 1705 and 1708.

The Trotts were a family whose name appears on the parish books all through. As far back as 1671, one

Frances Trott and her children, from St. Decumen's, came to reside at Ash Priors, and as usual, in spite of having at the time obtained the written word of the overseers to receive her back again, she had recourse to the justices of the peace to establish her claim. The Trott's, however, are still in the parish in 1725, when Luther Trott marries Sarah Blake. If we may do so, from the fact that Thomas Trott supplies strings for the bass viol in 1833, we infer that he was acquainted with the art of music and played that instrument in the village orchestra. There is evidence, too, that the Trotts were also skilled in another art besides that of music, since there is still in possession in the village an old clothes-brush made by one of that family with the name " Trott " worked in black bristles into the brush, and only quite recently has the name Trott died out in the parish.

Although they are becoming scarce, there are still some old heirlooms to be seen in the cottages, bits of old furniture and china. A memento of the Reform Bill of 1831 exists in the shape of a small jug, which has upon it various designs. Upon a pedestal stands a figure of a man with a mirror in his hand, upon which is the word "Truth." Upon the pedestal is written "Reform, Disfranchise, stone walls and parks. Give member to the People. King." On one side is a picture representing the King in act of dissolving Parliament. "My Lords and Gentlemen, I have been induced to resort to the measure for the purpose of ascertaining the sense of my people in the way in which it can be most constitutionally and authentically expressed. No! no! I hate reform !"

On the other side is a picture with figures of statesmen in state robes, holding up a scroll upon which are the names Grey, Brougham, Russell Althorp, Burdett, Norfolk and many other good fellows. "We are for the King. The people, the bill, the whole bill, and nothing but the bill. God save King William."

If this jug is not itself a valuable work of art, at any rate the designs upon it render a date unnecessary. It is obviously 76 years old and is an historic specimen of Bristol ware of the period, having survived the ravages of time, and the fate of the majority of little jugs.

SOME OLD CUSTOMS.

BLESSING THE APPLE TREES.

OF the old customs which still exist in the country a large proportion may be traced to pre-Christian times when the sacrifices to the gods of the fields and trees were important celebrations in the middle of the winter solstice. The earth was then perhaps covered with snow or ice bound. The grain was lying dormant, the fruit trees leafless, and our primitive ancestors offered up sacrifices to the tutelary guardians of their pastures and orchards in gratitude for past crops and in hopes that they might be still further or at least equally blest in the ensuing year. One of the survivals is the quaint custom of greeting the apple trees which used to be regularly observed in the West of England. The parishioners walk in procession, visiting the principal orchards of the parish. In each orchard one tree was selected as the representative of the rest, this was saluted with a certain form of words which have in them the form of an incantation. They then sprinkled the tree with cider, or dashed a bowl of cider against it, to ensure its being plentiful the next year.

> Here's to thee, old apple tree,
> Hats full, pecks full, great bushel bags full;
> Hurrah! Hurrah! Hurrah!

Ash Priors is full of orchards in which the people take the greatest interest and from which they derive

no small profit, and the parishioners still walk in
procession on the 17th January, visiting the principal
orchards of the parish and shouting several verses in
which occur similar words:—

> Pray to God they may bloom,
> Pray to God they may bear,
> That we may have apples
> And cider next year.
> Hurrah! Hurrah! Hurrah!

THE PRIDE OF SANDHILL.

The mistletoe (*Viscum album*), grows freely in the
orchards, and upon a species of Poplar common in the
place, called the black poplar (*populus nigra*), and is a
conspicuous object in winter time when the trees are
bare; also in Taunton market at Christmas time. It
is also found sometimes growing upon oaks and limes,
and even upon white thorn, but it is particularly fond
of the apple and the black poplar. We know that the
ancient Britons regarded the oak as a sacred tree, and
its mistletoe was doubly so. At the period of the winter
solstice a great festival was celebrated, and the mystic
parasite gathered with pomp and ceremony. Sallying
forth with their priests, the Druids, the Arch Druid,
robed in white, climbed the sacred tree and with a
golden sickle cut the mistletoe, which fell untouched
into the white robes of the attendant priests. Each
household received a spray of the sacred plant, to hang
over the entrance of their dwellings, whereby all evil
spirits were exorcised and no ill luck could enter the
house thus protected. There is a well-known benefit
club called "The Ancient Order of Druids," to which
a great number of men in this neighbourhood belong.
On club day they perambulate the parish with their

band and gorgeous banner, the office bearers dressed in
long white garments and wearing false beards. It has
often been a puzzle to me why they called themselves
Druids, and in reply to questions all the answer I have
got has been, " It is merely the name of the club."
" What's in a name? " Doubtless, it had its origin
in the spray of mistletoe which served as a charm to
keep off sickness, among other things, and in the
general knowledge of the medicinal properties of plants
possessed by the Druids.

THE ASHEN FAGGOT.

The yule log is no longer burnt upon the wide open
hearth. There is only one such hearth remaining in
the village and that in the little old cottage which
goes with the Vicarage. But still from the big houses
the rich send forth portions to the poor and keep up
the custom which is remembered of the kind lady,
Miss Winter, who, when living at the Priory, at
Christmas time sent round a piece of beef and a garment
for each of the old people in the parish and a bun
for each child in the school, to be distributed by the
Vicar; but as I passed the Inn one Christmas Eve I
noticed a very neat little faggot at the door and upon
enquiry I was told that it was made up of ash wood
and that the custom was to burn it on Christmas Eve,
and the saying was, " That as soon as the green band,
which bound it together, burst, it was time to have
a drink "; obviously the inevitable drink which accom-
panies all these ancient customs would not be long
delayed. It may be very interesting to keep an account
of these old customs, but very doubtful if it is advisable
to revive them. Thinking I was going to get a clue
to the origin of burning the ashen faggot I wrote to

the *Wellington Weekly News* office for a copy of a paragraph which appeared in their paper relating to it, but was much disappointed to find it only referred to a case before the Petty Sessions in consequence of keeping up the old custom, in which it appears that after the band burst the landlord of the inn was in the habit of standing free drinks all round.

In summing up the case the Chairman said "the custom was undoubtedly a bad one, but they were agreed that the permission of drunkenness could not be brought home to the defendant"; that under the peculiar circumstances of that night the wonder was that all did not get into such a state of helplessness that not one of them could be found to take the others home.

An innocent custom is that kept up by the school children on Shrove Tuesday, who, after school, go round shouting a little rhyme :—

> Dummery, dummery, dinky dough,
> Give me something and I will go,
> Off with the kettle, and on with the pan,
> Please give me something to put in my hand.
> Shrove Tuesday, Shrove Tuesday,
> My father went to plough ;
> My mother made pancakes
> She did not know how ;
> She turned them, she burned them,
> She made them quite black ;
> She put too much pepper
> And poisoned poor Jack.

Formerly they carried bags slung round their necks into which the cooks at the great houses put pancakes.

THE CRUEL MOTHER.

Among the folk songs from Somerset gathered by Mr. C. J. Sharp and C. L. Marson, the words and

air from Mrs. Eliza Woodberry, of Ash Priors, I find
this ancient ballad.

> There was a lady dwelt in York;
> Fal the lal the di-do;
> She fell in love with her father's clerk,
> Down by the green wood side O.
>
> She laid her head against a stone;
> Fal the lal the di-do;
> And there she made most bitter moan,
> Down by the green wood side O.
>
> She took a knife both long and sharp;
> Fal the lal the di-do;
> She stabbed her babes unto the heart,
> Down by the green wood side O.
>
> As she was walking home one night;
> Fal the lal the di-do;
> She met those babes all dressed in white,
> Down by the green wood side O.
>
> She said, " Dear children, can you tell,
> Fal the lal the di-do;
> Where I shall go, to heaven or hell?
> Down by the green wood side O."
>
> " O yes, dear mother, we can tell;
> Fal the lal the di-do;
> For its we to heaven and you to hell,
> Down by the green wood side O."

A Court Leet.

Mr. Jeboult in his history of Somerset tells us that a
Court Leet was formerly held at Ash Priors. This gives
the parish an importance which it would not otherwise
have had, for it signifies that Ash Priors was the
centre where the Court Leet of the manor was held
by the Steward of the Lord of the Manor for the
purpose of administering justice and preserving the

peace of that particular district. This court would be
subordinate to the Court Leet of the hundred which
was usually held by a bailiff or steward of the Sheriff
once a year, and that court in turn would be subordinate to the court of the High Sheriff of the county
who would go on circuit three times a year, for the
purpose of holding the great Court Leet of the county.

The Court Leet or law day was one of the most
ancient tribunals of the common law, having jurisdiction
over such offences as murder, treason, manslaughter
and all felonies at common law. Its duties were also
to inquire into questions of nuisances, disturbances,
and encroachments and to examine weights and
measures. The business of this court, as well as that
of the Sheriff's tourn or circuit, is now carried on by
the justices of the peace at the quarter sessions.

A REVEL.

There was a revel, according to Mr. Jeboult, on
the 14th day after Whit Sunday at Ash Priors. This
revel was probably in connection with the ancient
custom of holding church ales. The church ale, or
Whitsun ale as it was called, was an institution which
flourished in the sixteenth and seventeenth centuries.
It gives one a shock to hear of a revel in connection
with the holy season of Whitsuntide. Yet these ales
were much used for raising funds for repairing the
Church. Two men were chosen to act as masters
of the feast and called on every family in the village
to collect malt for brewing and corn for baking.
Sometimes a pastoral play was performed by the
villagers who expected no pay for their acting beyond
refreshments. There would be what were called
Morris dances, with six or so dancers, in which the

young women danced for a prize, which would consist of a piece of dress material, whilst the men engaged in boxing and wrestling matches. But, as the name "church ales" implies, drinking was one of the principal amusements.

It was at these revels that the English people showed their natural love for games, and, for want of better organization and patronage which they receive in the present day, the people of those days descended to the cruel and degrading instinct which finds pleasure in watching bull baiting and cock fighting.

Conclusion.

When we read the history of our ancestors, it seems to be principally a tale of woe and a record of crimes. Even the story of the monasteries, as told by other writers, gives a very different impression to that which Mr. Hugo has left for us in his history of Taunton Priory. The old historian, at least, loves to dwell on the worst side of the picture, and the names leave the impression that everyone was either a villain or a rogue, or a thief or a vagabond, and all sorts of immorality was prevalent. But it was not entirely so. Our Churches alone stand as evidences that those who handed them down to us were conscientious about their religious duties. There was a reverse side to the picture, and Mr. Marston has given a pretty description of village life at the beginning of the last century as seen through the taxed window. What he says applies to Ash Priors as much as any other country village. "The noise of the spinning wheel would drown all conversation, if any one had time to talk. Whilst the women are spinning wool into coarse cloth, for they made nearly all their own cloth and linen, the father of the family is making a pair of boots with the leather he has tanned himself, out of the skin of the old cow he killed last autumn, because it was likely to die of old age. Its beef is a trifle tough, but there are two sides of bacon hanging in the chimney, and the two don't go badly together. One of the grown up sons is carving spoons and platters to eat the beef and bacon with. Another is riveting a new bottom to his horn mug and hopes to mend the hole in the leather jug in time for it to be filled with ale from the brewing kettle for supper. The farm servants are sitting round the table with their master all equally busy making and repairing tools for next season's farm work. One is fitting a new handle to a scythe, or a fan to a flail; another is making willow or ashen teeth for the rakes, and hardening them in the fire. The girls have no time to read penny dreadfuls. One is plaiting wicker baskets; another, straw for the neck collar of the cart mare. Another is peeling rushes (grown on the Common) and dipping them into the fat to make candles of them. All are busy, happy and contented."

And if so then, surely now, from the impression left on the mind of the Lord Bishop of the Diocese, who, on the 4th December, 1907, made his visitation of the parish, and after listening to a report read by the Vicar, sitting in his chair at the Chancel Steps, left it on record in the book, that "Ash Priors was a parish to which great blessings had been vouchsafed."

INDEX.